Promoting Children's Learning from Birth to Five: Developing the New Early Years Professional

Second edition

Angela Anning and Anne Edwards

Open University Press

Open University Press
McGraw-Hill Education
McGraw-Hill House
Shoppenhangers Road
Maidenhead
Berkshire
England
SL6 2QL

email: enquiries@openup.co.uk
world wide web: www.openup.co.uk

and Two Penn Plaza, New York, NY 10121-2289, USA

First published 2006

A catalogue record of this book is available from the British Library

ISBN-10: 0335 219 705
ISBN-13: 9 780 335 219 704

Library of Congress Cataloguing-in-Publication Data
CIP data applied for

Typeset by BookEns Ltd, Royston, Herts.
Printed in Poland by OZGraf S.A.
www.polskabook.pl

Promoting Children's Learning from Birth to Five: Developing the New Early Years Professional

Sec

Contents

Introduction

In many ways the first edition of this book, published in 1999, was ahead of its time. The project that inspired us to write the book was about reshaping early years services into integrated delivery systems. Early years workers, wherever they are based and however different their roles, have demanding jobs. Current emphases on multi-agency teamwork and sharing professional knowledge have added to these demands and have highlighted the diverse training and experiences of early years professionals. We believe that the rich mix of professional expertise found in the provision of children's services is a strength to be tapped.

The research project that underpins this book demonstrates the strength of the mix of expertise in educational, childcare and family support services. It shows how professionals from a university, three local authorities (regional government agencies in the UK) and a wide range of backgrounds and children's services settings worked together to develop materials and strategies to support very young children as learners.

The book has three major themes:

- an exploration of the development of a *community of understanding* through a research partnership in England between regional government officers, practitioners responsible for delivering children's services and university-based early years specialists;
- an examination of how practitioners who work from evidence across professional boundaries are able to give strong, interactive and sensitive support to young children and their parents as they learn;
- a focus on children as learners from birth to 5 as they learn to become people who want to learn.

Our exploration of these themes brings us to consider ways of working with parents; how to promote inter-professional collaboration; how to achieve sustainable, systematic change in children's services; current research on early literacy and mathematical thinking; and how to provide environments in which children and adults learn together.

The title of this book gives equal weight to the learning of young children and their significant adults. We are convinced that children learn most readily in contexts where parents and professionals are keen to learn. Early childhood provision has a strong professional base from which to develop joined-up thinking. In this book we explore the strength of that base. We found the blend of expertise available in our research partnership to be an exhilarating mix and are confident that, together, early childhood professionals can meet the challenges of reshaping children's services.

The book draws on a project we ran together and is an enterprise for which we are jointly responsible. We each took the lead on specific chapters and commented on each others' work in writing both the first and second editions. Angela Anning led on Chapters 1, 2, 5, 6 and 10 and Anne Edwards on Chapters 3, 4, 7, 8 and 9. Throughout the text we argue for collaboration and knowledge construction through joint activity. The project and the book have been such an experience for us.

We are particularly grateful to the following people for their collaboration and the knowledge they shared: Jean Barker, Jan Bell, Mary Brailsford, Maureen Brett, Vanessa Broadbent, Margaret Buckley, Cilla Carr, Angela Clarke, Margaret Clarke, Margaret Fairclough, Anne-Marie Graham, Jean Hayes, Julie Helm, Ann Langston, Jill Lee, Jackie Lincoln, Judy MacDonald, Maureen McGlynn, Andrea Nicholson, Randolph Prime, Irena Riley, Sonia Roberts, Basil Sage, Peggy Sleight, Fiona Taylor, Sally Threlfall and Irene Vickers.

We are also grateful to Deborah Brady, Nicky Hutchinson, Julie Foster, Pat Russell and Sarah Warm for the administrative and secretarial support for the project and related publications.

1 Setting the national scene

In an attempt to coordinate and improve a legacy of disparate and under-funded services for children (Pugh 2001) the Labour government has introduced a raft of reforms. As we enter a historic third term of a Labour government in England, the field of early childhood services is benefiting from an unprecedented flow of money and attention. However the agenda has widened to include all children, not just young children, within the remit of reform. In government documentation childhood encompasses children in pre-school, primary and secondary school phases.

Local authorities are charged with developing Children and Young Peoples' plans by 2006 and establishing Children Trusts or similar arrangements for allocating funding streams to all services for children by 2008. Each local authority will appoint a Director of Children's Services. There will be a unified inspection system for all children's services. The radical agenda for reform is set out in *Every Child Matters: Change for Children* (www.dfes.gov.uk.everychildmatters).

There are five key principles embedded in outcomes for all children central to the Children Act 2004: being healthy, protection from harm and neglect, enjoying and achieving, making a positive contribution and economic well-being (www.dfes.gov.uk). These five principles are becoming the new mantra in the children policy area in England.

A national *Childcare Strategy* (DfEE 1998a) has a target of developing 100,000 new childcare places for 2008 and a *Ten Year Strategy for Childcare* (DfES 2005) is promising an out-of-school childcare place for all 3 to 14-year-olds from 8 to 6 o'clock every weekday by 2010. Neighbourhood Nurseries for under-5s are funded by public/private initiatives in areas of poverty to provide childcare to release parents for training/work.

There is a universal part-time pre-school education entitlement for all 3- and 4-year-olds whose parents wish to take it up, with a statutory *Foundation Stage Curriculum* (DfEE/QCA 2000) for 3- to 5-year-olds in any setting claiming to offer pre-school education. There is also a framework to support the learning of birth to 3-year-olds, *Birth to Three Matters* (DfES 2002). These are likely to be combined into one curriculum framework for birth to 5-year-olds.

Every local authority is required to appoint an officer responsible for coordinating services for children. The focus is to be on multi-agency delivery of services requiring all agencies, including Health Authorities, to share information and assessment frameworks and to plan together funding streams and early intervention strategies.

By 2008 in the 20 per cent most deprived areas in England 1,700 Children's Centres are to be created. These are to be modelled on Early Excellence Centres which were set up in the 1990s to pilot integrated services for young children and their families. The long-term plan is for a Children's Centre or Extended School to be established at the heart of every community. Extended Schools will be charged with providing such facilities as 'wrap around' care for children before and after school, a base for the delivery of integrated services and holiday playschemes.

Dealing with the volume and pace of change has been taxing for early childhood practitioners. For them the last decade has been both the best and worst of times! Policies on integrated children's services, establishing multi-agency teams and curriculum innovation have been mainstreamed in advance of the results of evaluations of their effectiveness on the assumption that the policies 'work'. We argue that it is not possible to translate current exemplifications of policy into practice without an understanding of their historical/sociocultural precedents (Cooter 1992). So in Chapter 2 we will discuss in more detail the processes by which early years services have pioneered pathways to integrated service delivery and 'joined up thinking' across the traditional disciplines of social services, education and childcare.

The historical/sociocultural influences on services for children

Bronfenbrenner's (1979) seminal ecological model of human development for understanding helps us to understand how young children are situated as learners by the societies in which they live. Bronfenbrenner argued that too little attention has been paid to 'the person's behaviour in more than one setting' or 'the way in which relations between settings can affect what happens within them' or 'the recognition that environmental events and conditions outside any immediate setting containing the person can have a profound influence on behaviour and development within that setting' (p. 18). He also argued that the developing person is an *active* agent in the environment, 'a growing dynamic entity that progressively moves into and restructures the milieu in which it resides' (p. 21) and that 'the interaction between a person and environment is viewed as two-directional, that is characterized by *reciprocity*' (p. 22, emphasis added).

As his thinking developed Bronfenbrenner updated his ecological model to place more emphasis on the bioecological and psychological aspects of children's development. He placed the child as a biosystem at the centre of his model (Bronfenbrenner and Ceci 1994) while retaining the overall integrity of his original version.

Bronfenbrenner's model defines a complex hierarchy of systems in which individual interactions between people are nested. The *micro-system* is the immediate setting in which a child may be at any one time. Particular activities and objects (physical features) will characterize that setting or environment and people will be assuming particular roles there. So, as we have seen, a child in a childcare setting is likely to be absorbed into different kinds of roles from those he or she will encounter in a pre-school. The next level is the *meso-system* and it consists of the networks or relationships between the settings in which a child finds itself at a particular point in her or his development. The networks between home and the child's playgroup experiences or between the child's parents, childminder and private pre-school arrangements are examples of meso-systems. The *exo-system* is the level in which the meso-systems are nested but which does not involve the developing person as an active participant. The exo-system would include the community in which particular children's services are developed and, for example, patterns of employment. There are likely to be variations in the evolution of services from one area to another because of the characteristics of their particular communities and patterns of employment. Finally, the *macro-system* is the overall cultural/political/social/historical setting in which the other systems are nested. So, we can see how complex and multifaceted the environmental influences upon young children really are. Figure 1.1 presents a version of the Bronfenbrenner model in diagrammatic form.

International perspectives on services for young children

Bronfenbrenner (1979) argued in his ecological model of child development that societies should place a high value on responding to the needs of young children. But he also argued that this can only be achieved when members of that society acknowledge the complex interrelationship between children, parents, educators, carers, community groups, those with responsibility for employment and housing, etc. In turn, priorities for allocating money to particular aspects of family needs – including the provision of children's services – depend crucially on the value systems of the dominant groups that determine social policy and allocate funding to community or welfare services. It is useful to remind ourselves that there are different models of

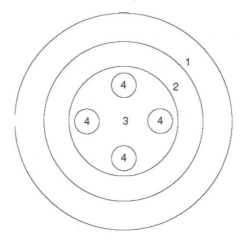

4 Micro-system: for example, the playgroup, pre-school education, childcare or childminder setting where the child experiences a particular pattern of activities, roles and interpersonal relationships.

3 Meso-system: interrelations between two or more settings in which the child actively participates – for example, home and nursery, childminder and playgroup.

2 Exo-system: settings that do not involve the child as an active participant but in which events occur that affect, or are affected by, what happens in the micro-systems – for example, local authority systems or inspection structures.

1 Macro-system: historical/social/cultural/ecological environments at national policy level.

Figure 1.1 Historical/cultural influences on services for the developing child based on Bronfenbrenner (1979)

provision for young children in other cultural contexts and to point out the features of two as exemplars from other countries: Denmark and New Zealand.

In Denmark there is a long-standing tradition of prioritizing funding to maintain high-quality services for young children and almost all children in the birth to 7 age group attend some form of daycare (David 1993). The concepts of social responsibility and democratic decision-making are high priorities in Danish cultural life. Through committee structures, local communities have far more involvement in managing services for children than in the UK. It is these committees that are charged with approving and regulating both childminding and centre-based daycare for children under 3. For 3- to 6-year-olds there are kindergartens within most localities as part of neighbourhood network systems. Most of them have extensive outdoor playground areas available for the children to play in throughout the day. There are also 'forest kindergartens' to which parents and carers may take children. In these centres the children spend most of the day – winter and summer – playing in the forests supported by a good adult:child ratio of 1:6 for 3- to 6-year-olds. Many kindergartens are open from 7 a.m. to 5 p.m. Children benefit from a 'coordinated school start' with staff from the two years of a feeder kindergarten liaising with those from Grades 1 and 2 of the primary school. Significantly the workers in the kindergartens are called 'pedagogues' but the approach to promoting children's learning is predominantly through play. The basic training of the pedagogues takes three and a half years.

Moss (1992: 33–4) praised the high quality of provision in Denmark: 'Denmark is in every respect exceptional … is the only EC (European Community) country where publicly funded provision accounts for most of the children in this age group (0–6) who attend some form of early childhood service.' With these kinds of values underpinning provision of services, it is no surprise that early childhood practitioners from the UK who visit Denmark's pre-school settings come back gasping with surprise at the quality of the provision they see – the purpose-built centres, high standards of resources, advantageous staffing ratios. Above all it seems to be the calm informality and physical freedom of the young Danish children, particularly in the forest kindergartens, that is the most striking feature of their daily lives in nursery settings for visitors from the UK.

In New Zealand early childhood services are primarily community based (Cullen 2001). They include sessional kindergartens, play-centres (parent cooperatives), childcare, Nga Kohanga Reo (Maori immersion centres), Pacific early childhood centres, coordinated family daycare and the correspondence school early childhood service. It is immediately evident from this list of provision that the concepts of respecting diversity within the complex demographics of New Zealand are central to their service provision. The New Zealand bicultural curriculum for all pre-school settings, *Te Whariki* (MoE 1996) is world famous. The view of children embedded in the curriculum is of a 'competent learner and communicator'. The four central principles – empowerment/*whakamana*, holistic development/*kotahitanga*, family and community/*whanau tangata* and relationships/*nga hononga* – reflect a holistic approach to children's learning, unlike the subject basis of the English curriculum. *Whariki* or mat signifies the weaving together of the central principles into five strands: well being, belonging, contribution, communication and exploration. The emphasis in translating the principles into practice is on learning through play. Again visitors to settings in New Zealand from the UK are struck by the quality of outdoor play experiences and the amount of choice the children are given in activities.

A second innovative and influential aspect of New Zealand practice is their approach to assessing children's development through learning stories (Carr 2001) which focuses on carefully documenting children's achievements in the specific contexts of their group settings, rather than, as in England, against predetermined objectives defined by a central government.

Throughout the 1990s attempts were made to integrate care and education. In 2002 *Pathways to the Future:Nga huarahi aratiki* (MoE 2002) set out a ten-year strategy for expanding early childhood services, upgrading their quality and promoting collaborative relationships between providers and their communities. There is currently an imperative to train all staff working with young children up to graduate status.

The research project

The two-year period of the research project (January 1997 to September 1998) was a challenging time for those working in and for services for young children in the United Kingdom. For the first time a curriculum framework, *Desirable Outcomes for Children's Learning on Entering Compulsory Education* (DfEE/SCAA 1996) had been introduced to all settings in England and Wales catering for 4-year-olds. The settings included state funded pre-schools, often called nursery schools in the UK (for 3- to 5-year-olds), nursery classes attached to primary schools (for 3- to 4-year-olds), voluntary sector playgroups (for 2- to 4-year-olds), childcare and family centres in the state sector for birth to 4-year-olds, independent schools (for 3- to 11-year-olds) and private daycare nurseries (for birth to 4-year-olds).

At this time pre-school education in state funded settings was free for children under 5. Parents paid modest fees per session for their children to attend playgroups. Nursery schools and classes and playgroups offered half-day (part-time) pre-school education for 3- and most 4-year-olds, offering some 4-year-olds full day schooling. The curriculum framework included six areas of learning: personal, social and emotional; language and literacy; mathematics; knowledge and understanding of the world; physical development; and creative development. In fact, other than personal, social and emotional development, the curriculum model replicated the English National Curriculum subjects for 5- to 7-year-olds of English, mathematics, science, geography, history, physical education, design and technology, art and music.

There was considerable anxiety among early years practitioners in all types of settings, but particularly those in the care sector, about putting the new curriculum framework for pre-school education into practice and about preparing for the system of national inspections set up to monitor its implementation. Anxiety was further exacerbated by the introduction of a statutory baseline assessment requirement from September 1998 for all primary schools. Baseline testing of children leaving their pre-school settings was focused on their achievements in English, mathematics and personal and social development. These national policy changes meant that in 1997–8 curriculum development, especially in literacy and mathematics, was high on the agenda of the development plans of the majority of group settings for children under 5 in England.

The research project was funded by the departments in three local authorities with responsibility for supporting children's services. The aim was to bring together expertise from key practitioner researchers from a range of education, childcare and family support service settings, with university-based researchers, to develop and articulate a curriculum model for effective education for very young children. Because of high levels of anxiety about achieving the Desirable Learning Outcomes, we were asked to focus on developments in literacy and mathematics. However our brief was that curriculum development was to be conceptualized within a holistic approach to developing learning from birth to 5. In particular the project foregrounded personal, social and emotional aspects of development as well as literacy and mathematics.

The project objectives were to:

- describe what strategies early years practitioners use to take advantage of what young children bring to pre-school learning contexts;
- identify strategies for the involvement of parents/carers as active partners in young children's care and education;
- identify what organizational features of early childhood services learning contexts maximize the quality of curriculum experiences offered to young learners;
- explore the processes by which professional knowledge is exchanged within multi-agency teams responsible for delivering children's services;
- define the features of adult/child and adult/adult interactions which are effective in promoting children's learning in pre-school settings;
- design curriculum literacy and mathematical development models for early childhood settings with exemplary materials for local contexts;
- develop a team of trainers capable of disseminating project findings at local, national and international levels.

Though the political and policy imperatives resulted in a focus on literacy and mathematics, the long-term aim was that the methods of working we were to trial would provide a model for the development of a broad curriculum for under-5s. Details of the curriculum model constructed between us will be given in Chapters 5 to 8. Details of the methodology of the research project will be given in Chapter 3.

The theoretical basis for this book draws on sociocultural psychology which emphasizes the relationships between individuals, actions, meanings, contexts, communities and cultural histories (see, for example, Chaiklin and Lave 1993; Wertsch *et al.* 1995; Cole 1996). These theories will be discussed in Chapters 3 and 4.

We also draw on Bronfenbrenner's seminal ecological model of human development (Bronfenbrenner 1979; Bronfenbrenner and Ceci 1994) we argue for the significance of the macro-system – the societal and cultural values and attitudes implicit in the way society organizes work, including children's services systems – for the micro-systems of adult/child/parent/carer interactions operating in settings catering for young children. Our evidence from the United Kingdom was that in the late 1990s, right at the start of a period of radical policy changes, the demands on early years professionals in translating government policy into practice were high. The lessons we learned from our project are highly relevant to understanding the dilemmas inherent in mainstreaming integrated children's services in the mid-2000s. However, first it is important to set out as a case the particular sociocultural-historical context in which our project operated in the 1990s. So it is to an account of these changes in policy and practice in pre-school education and childcare that we turn first.

Services for young children in England: the sociocultural context for the project

Pre-school education

In 1988 the Education Reform Act instigated a series of radical changes in the English and Welsh education systems. For the first time, schools were bound by statutory requirements for coverage of a centrally defined subject-based National Curriculum and related arrangements for testing. Statutory schooling was still deemed to begin at the age of 5. Key Stage 1 lasted from 5 to 7 years of age. However, early years educators responsible for the pre-school education of 3 to 4-year-olds were drawn into the reforms by whole school requirements to plan with colleagues within a subject-based model of learning. Increasingly they also had to conform to models of assessing, recording and reporting children's progress in subjects that were designed to ensure children's entitlement to continuity in education – a central plank of the policy arguments for curriculum reform.

In 1989 in the UK a House of Commons Select Committee on *Achievement in Primary Schools* (HMSO 1989) recommended that part-time nursery education should be available to all 3- and 4-year-olds whose parents wished to access it. The committee debated the issue of changing the statutory school starting age of 5 years, but decided to retain it. They acknowledged that, where no pre-school classes were available, many children were entering primary school reception classes at the age of 4 where they were being taught in classes of 25 or more, often by teachers unqualified in the education of under-5s. The committee recommended that additional funding should be provided in such reception classes to bring the staff/children ratios of 1:13 and funding for resources (including outdoor play space and equipment) up to 'pre-school education' standards.

The Select Committee recommendations were ignored as more and more children entered full-time schooling at age 4 as a cheaper option for the government to funding nursery education. Moreover, because government policy on the expansion of services for under-5s was advisory rather than statutory, local authorities were able to respond arbitrarily to recommendations to improve pre-school provision.

In 1999 a Literacy Hour (DfEE 1998b) and in 2000 a Numeracy Hour (DfEE 1998c) were introduced in primary schools in England and Wales and taught in most reception classes for 4-year-olds. These were aimed at raising standards in the basics in primary schools. The literacy and numeracy strategies resulted in more whole-class teaching, ability grouping, direct instruction and subject-based teaching for 4- to 7-year-olds (Pollard *et al.* 1994). Reception class teachers were confused about appropriate pedagogy for 4-year-olds (Taylor Nelson Sobres with Aubrey 2002) and how to use play for learning (Bennett *et al.* 1997).

Even at the time of our project in the 1990s research evidence had accumulated showing inappropriate levels of staffing, pedagogic practices, curriculum activities, physical space and equipment for 4-year-olds in schools (Bennett and Kell 1989; Cleave and Brown 1989, 1991a, 1991b; Pascal 1990) and official reports were emphasizing the importance of high-quality pre-school education (DfES 1990; Ball 1994). In 1999 in response to anxieties about the 'too formal too soon' approach to educating 4-year-olds (Sylva 1994), the Foundation Stage curriculum, with Early Learning Goals, was introduced. The Foundation Stage curriculum model replicated the six areas of learning of the Desirable Learning Outcomes. The guidelines for achieving the Early Learning Goals were more principled than those for achieving the

Desirable Learning Outcomes. They referenced the importance of professionals working in partnership with parents, of children learning through play and of striving for a balance between adult- and child-initiated activities in promoting children's learning. Many local authorities set up Early Years Units in primary schools combining the resources, space, staffing and outdoor play facilities of pre-school and reception classes for part-time nursery education for 3-year-olds and full time for 4-year-olds.

In 2002 a framework, *Birth to Three Matters* (DfES 2002), was introduced for the learning needs of under-3s. It was based on four aspects of development: a strong child, a skilful communicator, a competent learner and a healthy child. Guidance notes emphasized the importance of the reciprocity in carer/parent and child relationships and interactions.

Early models of assessment of the arrangements for delivering a National Curriculum to 5- to 7-year-olds had emphasized the importance of formative teacher assessments (TAs) on a regular basis in classrooms (DES 1988). These were to operate alongside the formal assessment requirements, the standard assessment tasks (SATs), to be administered in primary schools at the end of Key Stage 1 (for 7-year-olds) and Key Stage 2 (for 11-year-olds). Individual child attainments in all subjects of the National Curriculum had to be reported annually to parents. SATs results for English and mathematics (Standard Assessment Tasks in science were soon dropped) were aggregated for state schools and published as league tables in local newspapers. Private schools did not have to submit their results for publication. It was not surprising that headteachers of primary schools became preoccupied with raising standards in literacy and numeracy or that the emphasis in schools was on summative rather than formative assessment (Gipps 1994). It was to take until 2005 for SATs to be replaced by TAs for 7-year-olds. The change was the result of both parent and practitioner anxiety about the pressure on young children to take 'exams' so early and in response to narrowing the curriculum by teaching to the tests.

Baseline Assessment for children as they entered school (often at the age of 4) was made compulsory in 1999. Initially Local Authorities were allowed to use any of 90 baseline assessment schemes accredited by central government against criteria ensuring that literacy, mathematical development and social/emotional development were assessed. But it soon became clear that the results of these disparate schemes were of little value in determining the 'value-added' of Key Stage 1 schooling (Tymms 1999). In 2002 a standard, central government baseline assessment was made statutory for all 5-year-old children reaching the end of the Foundation Stage curriculum. These assessments were made as a result of detailed observations, mostly by qualified teachers working in Early Years Units or in Reception classes offering the Foundation Stage to 4-year-old children in their first year at primary school.

Meanwhile practitioners in early years settings were continuing to operate a variety of detailed profile records of individual children. In 2004 the introduction by the government of a detailed profile (QCA/ DfEE 2004) for each child, based on the 'stepping stones' of the Foundation Stage met with some resistance from practitioners.

In the absence of coherent central government or local authority policies on pre-school provision, playgroups and independent pre-schools continued to open where there was local demand. The provision was very different in these two types of settings. The independent sector tended to cater for parents who were willing to pay for their children to be educated in particular ways: for example using Montessori, Steiner or Froebel based approaches (see Anning 1997, Chapter 1) or formal traditional approaches to learning.

In contrast the Pre-School Playgroups Association, begun in the 1960s, provided a support system for many parents, almost always women, to establish playgroups offering part-time, low-cost places for pre-school aged children in rented premises. These were usually shared with other voluntary organizations such as youth clubs, cubs or brownies, or took the form of church or village halls and latterly the spare classrooms of primary schools. The Pre-School Playgroups Association, now the Pre-School Learning Alliance, grew into an influential lobbying group in its own right as women became empowered by working together, under severe financial and practical constraints, to fill the gaps left by inept government leadership in pre-school services. As facilities were expanded in primary schools for under-5s, a knock-on effect was that playgroups and nursery schools and classes were left to provide for a much younger population of 2- and 3-year-olds in order to stay in business. Managers and grassroots practitioners had to adjust rapidly to accommodate the younger 'clientele' with different staffing ratios, resources, curriculum activities, grouping arrangements and styles of adult/children interaction.

In 1997 within weeks of being newly elected the Labour government published a significant White Paper, *Excellence in Schools* (DfEE 1997). The paper proposed clear targets within early childhood education for the year 2002:

- high-quality education for all 4-year-olds whose parents want it;
- an early years forum in every area, planning childcare and education to meet local needs;
- a network of early excellence centres to spread good practice;
- effective assessment of all children starting school.

Each local authority was required to set up an Early Years Development and Childcare Partnership (EYDCP) (DfEE 2001a) representing the full range of providers and users of early years education and care in the area. The EYDCPs were expected to operate independently of Local Authority infrastructures in order to give equal entitlement to the maintained, voluntary and private sectors in expanding provision, though in reality they were often heavily dependent on local authority systems. The partnerships were charged with reviewing the children's services currently available in their local authority area, drawing up early years development plans and expanding pre-school and daycare provision against government targets. Partnerships had to ensure that up to two and a half hours a day of pre-school education was provided for all 4-year-olds whose parents wished to take the places up. This entitlement for free part-time pre-school education was extended to 3-year-olds in 2004. Parents could choose any setting for their children's entitlement, provided the setting had been inspected against the demands of the Ofsted inspection systems as providers of pre-school education. Private and voluntary funded settings were subsidized by government to provide free pre-school education. Daycare fees continued to be means tested. Childminders, nannies and private providers of daycare charged 'market prices'. Concessions in the form of Working Family Tax Credits were introduced for working parents to recoup some of the costs of childcare.

The EYDCP plans were charged with demonstrating how, over time, pre-school education would be dovetailed with high-quality childcare. By 2004 EYDCPs were replaced by Children's Trusts with responsibility for commissioning children's services, with a more central Local Authority role in their functioning.

It is to childcare provision, where practitioners have experienced parallel dramatic changes in policy and practice to their colleagues delivering pre-school education, that we now turn.

Childcare

Increasingly patterns of employment have favoured women. As manufacturing industries declined, service industries expanded. Employers, seeking a more flexible, part-time, cheaper, non-unionized workforce found that women fitted more passively into such patterns of employment than men. Women also traditionally have better 'people skills' and that quality was both useful and profitable for industries serving the public at a face-to-face level. The shifts in employment trends have been gradual, but relentless. In communities where manufacturing industries had employed predominantly men, the loss of jobs, and subsequent upheavals in their family and social lives caused massive levels of stress, disorientation and anger for men. For women, recast as workers as well as mothers, the pressures to do both 'jobs' well were formidable. At the time of the research project in the late 1990s, half of women with children under 5 worked. These trends resulted in increased demands for daycare for young children.

There was also a steady rise in the number of single parents (re-labelled in New Labour speak as lone parents) to a level of 1.7 million in 1998, mostly women. In 1998 1 million of these were unemployed or inactive in work. New Labour policy was to wean lone parents off state benefits by getting them into work or training under the Welfare to Work initiative. The ideology underpinning these initiatives was that it was better for lone parents of young children to have independence from state provision and be offered opportunities to train or return to work as soon as possible. Particularly in urban areas this resulted in a further expansion of both daycare and before- and after-school care provision (HMSO 1998). The latter became known as 'wrap-around care'.

Daycare had traditionally been the responsibility of social services in the UK. In 1989 the Children Act (DoH 1991) set out new requirements for local authorities to provide services for 'children in need' and to register, inspect and review childcare services. The Act required local authorities to review services every three years jointly with education authorities and in association with health authorities, voluntary organizations and independent providers. The emphasis was on quality control and accountability both to funding agencies and to 'consumers' of services. Guidance was given on ratios of staff to children, room sizes and space, health and safety, record keeping, disciplining of children and equal opportunities issues. Practitioners tended to emphasize the development of children's language and social skills in the activities they provided.

In the guidance there was a strong emphasis on partnership with parents/carers and on the importance of offering parents choices in childcare. However, parental choice was limited by what services were available. Despite the aspirations of the flagship Labour policy in expanding childcare, *Meeting the Childcare Challenge* (DfEE 1998a), diversification of services did not result in coherent daycare provision across England. In 2004 the National Audit Office (NAO 2004) found that though 100,000 new childcare places had been created since 1998 provision remained erratic with, for example, 37 childcare places per 100 children in the south-west of England but only 22 per 100 in central London. The report also highlighted problems of high staff turnover, lack of business acumen in many providers and the difficulty of locating suitable premises.

There had been initiatives to increase the number of childcare places in areas of poverty and deprivation. For example a Neighbourhood Nursery Initiative was intended to bring together private companies and state funding to build daycare facilities in the most deprived areas of the country. However, patchy provision meant for many parents, whatever their income levels, moving their children from one service to another in frantic attempts to cope with the financial and practical demands of working and parenting. This resulted in an inherent instability in many very young children's daily lives.

Even when children stayed in the same setting, there was another feature of instability. Because of poor working conditions and low pay there was often a high turnover of staff in daycare settings so that children experienced frequent changes of carers. Research into the care and learning needs of children under 3 (Elfer *et al.* 2003) in daycare nurseries indicated that children have a right to bond with a key worker in a well-managed and resourced daycare system. Without this proviso, they argued that it was almost impossible for babies and staff to develop authentic emotional relationships. This was deeply worrying when, as we will argue in Chapter 4, children need close and consistent relationships with key adults in their lives in order to thrive both emotionally and cognitively. Research evidence accumulated in the United States of America of the impact on under 2-year-olds of attending poor quality daycare for more than 20–30 hours per week, in that they were likely to exhibit increased levels of aggression and noncompliance between the ages of 3 and 8 (NICHD 2004).

While expanding childcare provision, a further challenge for the Labour government was to ensure that services were of a high quality. In 2001 a unified inspection system, the Early Years Directorate based at the Office for Standards in Education (Ofsted), was set up to replace the dual system of inspection of pre-school education (by educational inspections) and daycare (by Social Services inspections). However, many argued that 'quality' in daycare provision was not simply about meeting minimum standards as defined in Ofsted inspection systems.

For example, in 2004 Melhuish (2004) reviewed the effects of childcare and the parameters of quality for the Daycare Trust. He offered the following key messages from research about what produces the greatest benefits to children looked after in daycare which by consensus was defined as good quality:

- well-trained staff committed to their work with children;
- facilities that are safe and sanitary and accessible to parents;
- ratios and group sizes that allow staff to interact appropriately with children;

- supervision that maintains consistency;
- staff development that ensures continuity, stability and improving quality;
- provision of appropriate learning opportunities for children.

In the second half of the 1990s the government funded exemplary settings called Early Excellence Centres (Bertram and Pascal 1999) to model integrated services for children under 5 and their families. By the turn of the century an expensive anti-poverty intervention programme called Sure Start was rolled out over a five-year period in the five hundred or so most deprived areas of England. In 2005 the government pledged to set up 2,500 Sure Start Children's Centres by 2008 as the hubs of services for families with children. Extended schools are to be at the hub of integrated services networks. These initiatives, which involve expanding pre-school education, childcare, health, employment and family support services, will be discussed in more detail in the next chapter.

In Bronfenbrenner's model shown at Figure 1.1, pre-school education and childcare are shown as distinct micro-systems containing the interactions between parents/children and staff. However, as we have argued throughout this chapter there is increasing political/policy pressure for systems to be integrated into one all-encompassing service on one site for children and their families. In Chapter 2 we will discuss the distinctiveness of English services as they have operated, their respective strengths and weaknesses and the possibilities for generating new models of children's services as, in line with government policy, we work towards their integration within Children's Centres and Extended Schools.

Suggested reading

For a general discussion of key issues in the field of early years education and care in the UK a good starting point is the third edition of *Contemporary Issues in the Early Years: Working Collaboratively for Children*, edited by Gillian Pugh, published by Paul Chapman in association with the Coram Family in 2001.

Dahlberg, Moss and Pence's book *Beyond Quality in Early Childhood Education and Care: Postmodern Perspectives* published by Falmer Press in 1999 looks at the values underpinning early childhood services in Sweden, Reggio Emilia, Canada and the UK.

Early Childhood Education: Society and Culture by A. Anning, J. Cullen and M. Fleer, published by Sage in 2004 develops a critique of early childhood education in Australia, England and New Zealand using a sociocultural theoretical approach.

Goldschmied and Jackson's (1994) *People Under Three*, published by Routledge is a substantial text focused on very young children in group childcare settings. Elfer, Goldschmeid and Selleck's book, published by Sage (2003), *Key Person Relationships in Nursery*, investigates adult/child relationships in group settings.

Two books, *Working with the Under-Threes: Training and Professional Development* and *Working with the Under-Threes: Responding to Children's Needs* are collections of articles edited by Lesley Abbott and Helen Moylett (1997a and b) on a range of issues in early childhood education and care. Both are published by Open University Press.

For a closer look at assessment and record keeping in early childhood settings in England see Drummond, M. J. (1993) *Assessing Children's Learning* (London: David Fulton) and in New Zealand, see Carr, M. (2001) *Assessment in Early Years Settings: Learning Stories*. London: Paul Chapman Publishing.

2 The integration of early childhood services

From disintegration towards integration: policy into practice

As we have discussed in Chapter 1 the construct of childhood enshrined in current English government legislation is children from birth to 18, rather than simply under-5s. However, during the period of the project, the emphasis in service reform was on early years settings. There were two major focuses of government policy for the delivery of services to young children and their families. First, policy shifted to the concept of the welfare and attainments of the child being nested within the social context of family and community. This kind of thinking is reflected in Bronfenbrenner's ecological model of child development referred to in Chapter 1. However constructs of childhood (James and Prout 1997), family (Smart and Neale 1999) and community (Barnes *et al.* 2004) were all undergoing profound changes. This means that policy makers and practitioners charged with delivering services are having to confront new challenges in order to respond to changing expectations of young children's entitlements, new versions of families and shifts in community characteristics and values.

A second imperative has been that in order to meet the needs of families with young children services should be 'joined up' and delivered by professionals working together in multi-agency teams. The imperative acknowledges the interrelated nature of family, parent and children's needs in the fields of health, social services, education, law enforcement and housing in recognition that people live 'joined up' lives. Radical changes are being imposed on the way local authorities in England structure and manage partnerships between agencies and services. Services will be expected to share information using common databases. There will be a common inspection framework. Local education authorities will in effect cease to exist, their power lost. Within the next decade, as is currently the case in Birmingham, generic Children's Services Authorities will be the norm. However, despite this major shift in policy, there are few conceptual frameworks for setting up, managing and defining new versions of professionalism in emerging multi-agency work practices.

The processes by which multi-agency teams deliver services are only just beginning to be documented in the UK (Anning, *et al.* 2006; Atkinson *et al.* 2002; Easen *et al.* 2000; NECF 2004).

'Community-led' decision-making is another well-used term in UK government policy. There is an assumption that professionals will be responsive to the expressed needs and demands of their client families in designing and delivering new versions of services. Underlying the mantra of community-led decision-making is a contrasting discourse from central government focusing on efficiency in resourcing services and their cost benefits to the State. There are expectations that families will use the opportunities offered by a raft of family and parental support initiatives to improve their diet, take up training and/or employment, and improve their families' physical and mental health. Parents are expected to support their children's early learning and cooperate with care and pre-school education settings to enhance their children's educational attainments.

However, the values and beliefs of professionals delivering services may be in conflict with those receiving them. There are distinct cultural preferences in families' life styles. For example, buying a diet of fast food with chips from the local chippie may be preferable to spending time and energy cooking carrots and stew for a large family. Watching television may be more satisfying and relaxing for many stressed parents than playing educational games with their children. Smoking in the comfort of your home may be a more manageable stress reliever than attending yoga sessions in a draughty church hall. More significantly each family, regardless of apparently 'common' characteristics of a community, brings to child-rearing a different set of beliefs about, for example, the roles of men and women in family life and employment and how to rear and discipline children. These differences may be particularly acute where poverty, rural life styles or diversity are features of communities (Anning 2005a).

Practitioners may find themselves trapped between competing imperatives: to respond to the expressed needs/preferences of their communities and to deliver against targets specified by the government as intended outcomes of reconfigured services. An example would be to reconcile the leisure/relaxation needs of stressed parents living in poverty with the government targets of getting them 'back' to work. Another would be balancing the emotional needs of babies for consistent, reciprocal care with the government imperative to get lone parents released from mothering to take up facilities enabling them to train for employability. Another would be to reconcile the perceived needs of particularly vulnerable groups (such as looked-after children) with their rights to make individual decisions about their own futures.

A further complication in operationalizing 'joined-up services' is that professionals from diverse fields of health, social welfare, education and childcare make up the multi-agency teams. These professionals are trained in different ways, have different working conditions and salaries, have different priorities and espouse different beliefs/values. However, little attention (at theoretical, empirical research or practical levels) has been paid to exactly how disparate groups of early childhood education and care and family support workers reconcile these differences. We do not know how they learn to share knowledge, gain understanding of each others' beliefs and ways of working and negotiate to present a shared vision of 'joined-upness' to their clients (Anning, *et al.* 2006; Atkinson *et al.* 2002; Edwards 2004a).

The policy shift towards integration of children's services has been a slow but relentless process. At the time of writing in 2005 every local authority in England is charged with bringing education, health, family support and child protection services together into generic children's services. But early years services were the pioneers of these changes. We will then explore what research evidence we have of the effectiveness of early childhood services in promoting the education, health and well-being of young children and their families in England (and, where work in the field has been seminal, in international contexts).

Even in the early 1980s misgivings had been expressed at macro-level political and policy forums about the effects of disparate administrative and accountability systems on access to education and care for the under-5s. For example, a report by Bradley (1982) argued that services for children and families should be better coordinated by establishing clear links between the various agencies, while accepting that they remain distinct. In 1988 the Early Childhood Unit published the results of a survey of systems of provision for young children in all local authorities. Despite interest among local authorities in working towards coordinating services, they reported that 'in the face of low resourcing, seemingly intractable problems over vested interests between departments, and often no clear sense of direction as to the best way forward' (Pugh 1988: 81) little progress was being made in putting their ideas into practice.

However, at the exo-system level some local authorities did set up pioneering family centres during the 1980s and 1990s where attempts were made to model coordinated services for young children and their families. An early account of the complexity of trying to combine the traditions and cultures of social services-based daycare and education-based school systems and ways of working is given in Ferri *et al.* (1981). Well-known examples of family centres that thrived despite the difficulties are Hillfields Nursery Centre in Coventry (the first to be established) and the now internationally known Penn Green Nursery Centre in Corby. These centres were offering flexible hours of daycare and pre-school education and, for example, access to health care services for children under one roof as 'one stop shops' as early as the 1980s. They were way ahead of national policy initiatives. In the 1990s the term 'educarers' was coined for the professionals working in these innovative contexts who combined care and education in their responsibilities for children. Family centres had a strong tradition of actively involving the local community, especially the parents of attending children, in their daily working. Many local authorities attempted to follow the early examples of innovative family centres by reshaping social services daycare nurseries into family centres. The centres offered users flexible care of children whose parents were working (often part time), respite care for families in crisis and family support for parenting.

In Strathclyde, the largest education authority in Scotland, a small number of existing pre-school nurseries and daycare settings were converted into 'community nurseries' offering flexible services for birth to 5-year-olds. In Scotland there was a much broader approach to inspecting pre-school education services for 'quality' than in England. In the 1990s the Strathclyde local authority invested strategically both in the evaluation of its initiatives to coordinate services and in the professional development of the staff responsible for implementing change. As the thorough and informative evaluation reports of the innovation show, attempts to combine the working conditions and lives of teachers and carers in one setting were problematic (Wilkinson 1994).

In the 1990s the discourse about English services shifted from talk of coordination to talk of integration. Pugh and McQuail (1995), based at the National Children's Bureau, produced a short publication to support an integrated approach to the planning and management of services for young children. They reported on a small-scale study of 11 local authorities where services were categorized as integrated, coordinated or collaborative. *Integrated services* were defined as unified under-5s services with a committee or sub-committee of the council with considerable delegated authority to develop the initiative of integration. *Coordinated services* were in authorities where there were significant formal arrangements between departments at member and officer level. *Collaborative services* were where there were few formal arrangements beyond the ordinary corporate management procedures of the authority. Pugh and McQuail argued that each of the local authorities studied were at a different point – determined by their political, geographical and historical circumstances – on the continuum of integration to collaboration. The authors argued persuasively that 'if the aim is for universal services offering care and education to all children whose parents want it, then an "integrated" approach appears to be most effective' (p. 16). However they offered no hard evidence for what 'most effective' meant in terms of outcomes for children, parents or families.

The National Children's Bureau commissioned an economist to estimate the costs of a comprehensive system of daycare and pre-school education and to suggest ways it might be funded (Holtermann 1992, 1995). Holtermann's analysis indicated that the costs of such provision – estimated at £2.7 million – would be offset by the savings gained from women coming off benefits to work and additional income generated from their employment through income tax and national insurance contributions. However, cost benefit analysis studies since this period have been notoriously complex and access to actual costs and measurable benefits of reshaping services for children has remained difficult (Tunstill *et al.* 2005).

In 1997 the three local authorities with whom we worked were all well along the continuum towards integration of their services; but it is important to recognize that they were operating within the macro-level national policies and imperatives outlined above. Large and unwieldy Early Years Development and Childcare Partnership committees grappled with the complex task of auditing needs and constructing Early Years Development Plans. In 1997, an Audit Commission report, *Counting to Five*, warned that many local authorities were struggling to comply with both the spirit and the practices of the new regulations on the education and care of young children. Particularly where local authorities had extensive services already, the voices of independent providers frequently were unheeded in forum debates. Only about half the authorities had formal systems for consultation with the private and voluntary sectors. As 4-year-olds entered reception classes, and council-run nursery classes opened in primary schools, playgroups, perhaps only half a mile from the schools, were forced to close as their numbers dwindled. The Audit Commission report also pointed out that the few nursery schools that did survive cost on average 50 per cent more than nursery classes in primary schools to run; but there was little evidence of authorities 'making better use of these facilities by expanding nursery schools' role' (Audit Commission 1997: 29). The report cited evidence of many vacant or underused places in the reception and nursery classes of schools. Though the take-up of day nurseries' places was reported to be healthy at 90 per cent, the report pointed out that ensuring children's regular attendance was problematic. Consequently erratic and poor attendance at day nurseries was identified as a 'value for money' issue.

How did the three local authorities with which we worked for the project fit into this national, macro-level context? If we return to Figure 1.1 of Bronfenbrenner's model on page 4 we are reminded that the working lives of each group of workers who came to the project were influenced by the macro-system of national policy and practice, but also by the links within the meso-systems developed within local authorities to cope with new legislation and government demands. There were differences within their infrastructures and systems based on their respective historical, political, social and economic contexts. However the three local authorities demonstrated common characteristics in approaches to integration. They had developed strategies for reviewing the quality of services that were 'owned' by elected members of committees, officers charged with managing new initiatives and to some extent the early years workers whose practices were to be monitored. They had extensive programmes of staff development at a range of levels for all categories of workers in early years settings. They had geared their 'vision statements' to local contexts and priorities. They had set up structures to manage the budgets which would deploy resources to settings at point of need. Despite these positive and forward-looking strategies, they all reported difficulties in grappling with relationships with key players in other sectors at various times during the period of change. Confronting professional jealousies, and often fiercely defended vested interests, was perhaps the most difficult part of managing change reported by the heads of services in the three local authorities. But this was true of early years partnerships across the country.

In the late 1990s the government funded over one hundred Centres of Excellence in England and Wales to model the delivery of high quality, integrated services for young children and their parents (DfEE 2001b). Funding for piloting the Centres of Excellence was generous. The initiative was evaluated at both local (Warin 2001; Anning 2005a) and national levels (Bertram and Pascal 2001; Bertram *et al.* 2002). Evidence of the effectiveness of the models was tentative – though in general parents were enthusiastic about using the centres. However, local evaluations evidenced the difficulties practitioners were having in redefining their professional identities as their roles and responsibilities changed within multi-agency teamwork. Nevertheless, government policy was to roll out the model by encouraging multi-agency service delivery for families with young children to be based on Sure Start Children's Centres (DfES 2004). The centres are designed to form the hub of educational, childcare, family support, training for employment and health service delivery. Concerns raised within the local Centre of Excellence evaluations about the complexity of managing change from distinct to integrated service delivery, even on the small scale of the well-funded pilot Centres of Excellence model, are likely to be experienced by a wide range of workers within the next decade in England as children's centres are set up nationwide.

Another major government initiative to model integrated services for families with children up to the age of 4, delivered by multi-professional teams, was exemplified in the multi-million pound (£1.4 billion over six years) anti-poverty initiative called Sure Start (www.surestart.gov.uk). Between 2000 and 2004 Sure Start Local Programmes were established in more than five hundred of the most deprived areas of England. There were seven Sure Start services principles: working with parents and children, services for everyone, flexible at the point of delivery, starting with babies before birth, respectful and transparent, community driven and professionally coordinated and outcome driven. Government prescribed targets for outcomes included a wide range of parent and child health aims, enhanced developmental progress for children under 4, community capacity building, enhanced employment and training opportunities for parents and enhanced quality of life for communities within the Sure Start areas. Members of staff were expected to work closely with local community members to identify priorities for services within their locality and plan to deliver them in ways that would engage parents, children and families, particularly those defined as 'hard to reach'.

The intervention is being evaluated (see www.ness.bbk.ac.uk). Findings from the evaluation of the implementation of Sure Start indicate that though many parents are enthusiastic about Sure Start, developing and managing integrated services in areas defined as 'deprived' has proved challenging. The challenges are in maintaining relationships with mainstream agencies with responsibilities for services while at the same time developing innovative services within a small, tightly defined geographical area. A second set of challenges is in developing multi-agency teamwork in delivering services where staff may come from very different working traditions and cultures. These differences create tensions as staff struggle to reconcile their own professional identities and knowledge domains with Sure Start requirements to work within multi-professional teams (Tunstill *et al.* 2005). So far the impact reported on children and parents is small, but some local programmes are promoting better outcomes (Melhuish *et al.* 2005) Another significant intervention to encourage collaborative working with children's services for 5- to 13-year-olds in England is the Children's Fund initiative. The evaluation produced insights into the development of interagency work. One of the early reports (NECF 2004) focused on collaboration between practitioners.

The effectiveness of types of provision for under-5s: research evidence

Before we are introduced, in Chapter 3, to the characters who worked with us on the project in the late 1990s, it is important to stand back from policy/practice issues and ask some hard-edged questions about research evidence we have of the *effectiveness* of types of early childhood provision and services. As the head of services in one of the local authorities pointed out to us, there are fiercely held beliefs at local and national levels of policy that some combinations or types of services for young children are better than others. But what research evidence is there to substantiate such beliefs? Do we know that integrated services will be more effective than the traditional distinct services for young children and their families?

Trying to tease out the significance of the available research evidence on the effects of pre-school experiences on young children's development is complex. In the first instance, we have to try to disentangle evidence about the effects on children of attendance at *types of settings* from evidence about the effects of the *quality of experiences* they had in those settings. The quality of experiences might include what kind of curriculum they experienced or the way in which adults behaved towards them while they were there. A third important feature of early childhood experiences away from home is the *involvement of parents* and the impact of continuities or discontinuities of adult/child relationships and behaviours in the two different areas of the children's daily lives.

In the UK, many young children experience several types of settings. For example, a child may have experience of a childminder, some playgroup sessions and then half days in a pre-school or early years unit before he or she starts school. So we have to take all these variables into account when trying to determine which experiences resulted in what effect on a child. It is difficult then to ascribe clear-cut cause and effect answers to questions about the impact of pre-school education and care experiences. However, we do have some research evidence which we will briefly review below. The 'Suggested reading' section at the end of the chapter should be of assistance to those wishing to pursue 'effectiveness' arguments.

Types of settings

The most influential study of the last decade has been the Effective Provision of Pre-School Education (EPPE) Project (Sylva, Melhuish *et al.* 2003), a longitudinal study funded by the Department for Education and Skills (DfES) from 1997 to 2003. The research explored the effect of children's attendance of pre-school centres on their cognitive progress and social emotional development. The sample included over three thousand children attending six types of pre-school provision between the ages of 3 and 5 (when they were mostly in reception classes or early years units in primary schools). The project is currently extended to track the children's progress in their primary schools from 5 to 7, when they reach the end of Key Stage 1 (for children aged 5 to 7 in English primary schools).

The research design included exploring the impact of a wide variety of children's experiences beyond their attendance at types of pre-school centres. Variables included parent and family characteristics and the home learning environment. Within the sample there was a group of children matched to the family/home characteristics of children attending centres who were home educated. This sub-sample acted as a control group. There were six types of pre-school settings: nursery class, pre-school playgroup, local authority daycare nurseries, private daycare nurseries, nursery schools and integrated centres (such as those at Hillfields and Pen Green described earlier). The small number of integrated centres in the EPPE centre sample included Early Excellence Centres. The settings were located in five regions across England representing a wide range of socioeconomic and geographical features, and including ethnically diverse and socioeconomically disadvantaged communities.

Variation in the quality of individual centres was explored using the Early Childhood Environment Rating Scale (ECERS-R) (Harms *et al.* 1998) and an additional educational schedule, ECERS-E (Sylva, Siraj-Blatchford *et al.* 2003). In addition the Caregiver Interaction Scale (Arnett 1989), an observational instrument, was used to provide measures of adult/child interactions.

The team measured the influences of different background factors and attendance at types of settings on children's attainments. The findings included a rich array of evidence about what was likely to predict children's cognitive and social emotional gains before they started formal schooling. Key findings were that high-quality scores on the ratings scales, linked to high-quality staff qualifications, predicted higher gains for children. Overall, children achieved better outcomes when they attended integrated centres or nursery schools. They achieved less well in private daycare nurseries and playgroups. Case studies of centres identified as particularly effective were carried out to explore the processes (such as the quality of adult/child interactions) within the centre activities and their possible relationship to children's attainments. Evidence from the case studies will be discussed in the next section of the chapter.

However, home factors were equally important in predicting children's gains. Where parents actively engaged in activities with their children, regardless of their socioeconomic circumstances or levels of education, children's intellectual and social development was enhanced. In other words, what parents did with their children proved to be more important than who they were.

Prior to the EPPE study there was some evidence of the impact of attendance at daycare centres on young children in England. A longitudinal study based at the Thomas Coram Research Unit of daycare arrangements for the first child of 255 families in London tracked their development up to the age of 6 by visiting them at home on four occasions (Melhuish 1991). The children were tested on language development and intelligence. They were observed both at home and in care settings. Their mother, carers and teachers completed questionnaires. Information was collected about the mother and her partner's work patterns and reasons for choices and changes in childcare arrangements. The results showed that children who experienced more changes in daycare arrangements had a slower rate of cognitive development during their first three years. However, in this study children who had been in daycare settings showed no more signs of problem behaviour than those who had been cared for at home.

Quality of daycare is measurable using parallel standardized schedules to the ECERs scales, the ITERs (Infant and Toddler Environment Rating Scales) (Harms *et al.* 1998). Domains for assessing quality include structural features (such as buildings, management and organization) and process variables (such as the quality of interactions within settings). Key structural variables identified by Phillips (cited in Hayes *et al.* 1990) are the 'iron triangle', because they are interrelated: staff qualifications and training, staff/child ratios and group size. These variables are routinely associated with positive, responsive adult/child interactions. In turn these are associated with positive outcomes for children's attainments as measured on developmental scales and parents' ratings of satisfaction with services.

Research into the effects of attendance at daycare settings has tended to focus on measures of emotional adjustment (see Sylva and Wiltshire 1993), probably because of residual anxiety about the effects of 'maternal deprivation' which had been so influential in Bowlby's work in the 1950s (Bowlby 1953). Bowlby argued that all children are biologically programmed to form an attachment to a primary carer. His studies of children in residential care indicated that children who had not enjoyed this attachment were unable to form lasting and meaningful relationships in later life. 'Attachment theory' has been particularly influential in research into the impact of attending daycare settings on child outcomes. More recent research has indicated that it is the quality of care, rather than the effect of care *per se*, that may have damaging effects on children's emotional adjustment. Poor-quality care in daycare settings, often characterized by care giving that is emotionally detached or inconsistent, results in children not having secure attachments to adults. There is research evidence from the USA that attendance at such poor-quality settings, particularly where children were from deprived home settings, is likely to result in children manifesting aggression and poor social emotional functioning at school entry (Belsky 1999). These are clearly important findings since the quality of relationships a young child establishes with his or her main carers lays the foundations of later social and emotional relationships. These foundations include young children's understanding of and ability to regulate their own emotions, as well as to make and break friendships, cope with conflicts and negotiate ways around disagreements. These issues will be explored further in Chapter 4.

In the next section we focus more closely on research evidence of the impact on young children of the quality of their experiences, rather than simply of attendance, at pre-school settings.

Quality of experiences

The most frequently cited research in the field of the effectiveness of pre-school curriculum/quality of learning experiences is the report on the long-term gains for children in the USA who were exposed to the High/Scope Curriculum in the Perry Pre-school Project. The High/Scope Curriculum is characterized by: high-quality, active learning experiences for children; a 'plan-do-review' sequence in the way children are encouraged to work supported by adult interactions; an adult/child ratio of 1:8; and close involvement of parents in the programme. Every parent of children involved in the pre-school programme had frequent visits from trained workers to ensure that there was consistency between the learning experiences offered within the programme and what parents did with the children at home. A seminal longitudinal study (Schweinhart and Weikart 1993) showed that children who had experienced the programme were more likely to achieve academically in school. More significantly, long-term monitoring of the children showed that as they grew up they had greater self-esteem, more realistic vocational plans and were prouder of what they had achieved. In adulthood they were less likely to be involved in crime, unemployment, teenage pregnancies or drug/alcohol abuse. (For a detailed account of studies of the effectiveness of pre-school research in the USA see Sylva 1994.)

Since 1993 a research and development project, 'Effective Early Learning' (EEL), led by Pascal and Bertram (Pascal *et al.* 1997) has focused on improving the quality of children's learning in all types of early childhood settings. The EEL framework 'Framework for Quality' is organized around ten dimensions of quality. Key foci of quality are embedded in a scale which measures children's involvement and adult engagement in learning episodes. The EEL project is heavily influenced by Laevers (1994) scales of children's involvement in activities, often play-based, as measures of effective learning environments. He argues that levels of involvement in play are integral to children's well-being and intellectual development. The Laevers scales include monitoring levels of adult involvement in children's play bouts. He draws attention to the importance of the emotional aspects of play and of adults acting as 'play partners' who are responsive to young children's interests and preoccupations.

The process features of high quality highlighted by the case studies in the EPPE project referenced in the section above tended to focus on the quality of 'educational' interactions associated with children's enhanced attainments in both cognitive and social-emotional outcomes. EPPE findings were that high-quality provision in settings was characterized by:

- adult–child interactions involving 'sustained shared thinking' and open-ended questioning;
- practitioners with a clear grasp of child development and good curriculum knowledge;
- shared educational aims with parents;
- formative feedback to children in learning episodes;
- transparency in behaviour policies and practice.

These findings are in line with the way we all worked with children and parents in the project. We will expand them as we describe what we did. In Chapter 4 we will emphasize in particular the importance of dispositions to learn which are developed in the important interactions between young children and key adults in their lives.

Summarizing insights from research: implications for integrated services for children

So research evidence does give us some insights into the effectiveness and/or appropriateness of both the types of provision and the quality of experiences for young children before they start school. In summary:

- the most effective forms of provision demonstrate close, working partnerships between parents and staff in the settings;
- there is a need to expand services for young children to match the changing needs and lifestyles of families and their patterns of employment;
- the most crucial features of high quality in any pre-school setting are the expertise and commitment of the staff and the quality of

their relationships and interactions with children and their parents;

- children who attend some form of pre-school provision achieve higher cognitive and social emotional levels of development before they start formal schooling;
- attendance at nursery schools and integrated centres appear to promote the highest gains on these measures;
- where children under 2 attend poor-quality daycare on a full-time basis they demonstrate higher levels of aggression and poorer social/emotional skills at the start of school;
- in particular children from disadvantaged backgrounds achieve better results at the beginnings of schooling if they have had experience of pre-school education or good-quality daycare.

Simply integrating services will not necessarily enhance the quality of provision for young children and their families in the UK, though in terms of equity it must make sense to offer families the benefits of flexible, affordable and accessible local services (Makins 1997). What really would make a difference to the quality of early years provision is a profound change in attitude in this country to the provision of services for children so that, as in Scandinavian systems as discussed in relation to Denmark in Chapter 1, it is taken for granted that society will value them and divert funding to them. We will return to the wider implications of a much more radical imperative to reshape children's services in England in the final chapter. The Labour government initiatives have certainly taken us in the right direction in policy. However changes in practice will only come about through the ambassadorship of the professionals working the field of early childhood services. It is to a discussion of their professionalism in a period of radical changes in their roles and responsibilities that we turn in Chapter 3.

Suggested reading

An accessible book on research evidence about the quality and effects of daycare, with references to studies in a number of countries, is Hennessy, E., Martin, S., Moss, P. and Melhuish, E. (1992) *Children and Day Care: Lessons from Research* (London: Paul Chapman Publishing).

Moss, P. and Penn, H. (1996) *Transforming Nursery Education* (London: Paul Chapman Publishing) offers a strong critique of existing services in the UK and a vision of how they might be in the future.

The EPPE team have published a series of reports on their research findings which are important sources for those interested in a deeper understanding of both their research methods and findings. You can purchase these from EPPE Project, University of London, Institute of Education, 20, Bedford Way, London, WC1H OAL. On the DfES website you will find Sylva, K., Melhuish, E., Sammons, P., Siraj-Blatchford, I., Taggart, B. and Elliott, K. (2003) *The Effective Provision of Pre-school Education (EPPE) Project: Findings from the Pre-school Period*. Brief No. RBX 15-03. London: Department of Education and Skills.

3   The inquiring professional

The importance of adults

The research on early education we outlined in Chapter 2 and the work on children's learning and development we discuss in Chapter 4 all point to just how important the quality of adult–child interactions and the context of those interactions are, if children are to be helped to see themselves as people who can and do learn easily.

When we planned the project on which this book is based we therefore focused on how the project would support pre-school practitioners as they in turn supported children as learners. We knew that the project had to deal with a number of challenges to professional practice already discussed in the previous chapters. In summary they were:

- the diverse nature of pre-school provision and the professional groups which contribute to provision, which between them draw on the professional cultures of health care, nursery nursing, social work, voluntary work and education;
- an emphasis on children's entitlement to educational provision which pre-school practitioners were obliged to meet;
- pre-school practitioners had to meet this entitlement while they were themselves developing new professional identities as both educators and carers.

While we planned the project we worked with three aims which we hoped would meet these challenges. The aims were ambitious and we were aware that our project could only be one small part of a much wider set of efforts aimed at creating an informed community of early educators. The three aims were:

1. the development of a new form of professional practice which drew on the best of current traditions of education and care;
2. the professional development of early education professionals;
3. some useful contributions to the knowledge base that informs the professional development of practice and practitioners.

These aims were particularly ambitious because the project started just as pre-school practitioners were beginning to get to grips with the curricular demands of an emphasis on the educational purposes of pre-school provision. Consequently the project itself became the vehicle through which practitioners met these new demands in their settings and developed some of the ideas that were to underpin their professional practices.

We were working with frameworks drawn from sociocultural psychology which drew our attention to the meanings given to the language and the materials used by practitioners. We were not initially using ideas from activity theory (Edwards 2005; Engeström 1999) which allows us to look at the relationship between practices and organizational dynamics. However, these issues will be addressed in Chapter 9 and have been outlined in some detail in relation to the present project in Edwards (2004b). In designing the project we were hoping to observe the development of common understandings when, for example, early literacy and numeracy were discussed, and to see an increased capacity to recognize the educational potential in familiar materials. We were particularly interested in focusing on how high-quality interactions between children and adults helped children to learn to enjoy learning. We were also aware that keeping parents and carers of the children centrally involved in deciding priorities for their learning was important.

The ideas on children's learning, early literacy and early mathematics used by practitioners in the project are outlined in Chapters 4 to 8 in this book. In this chapter we shall look at the wider project and its use of case study and action research; the individual action research projects of the practitioners; and the importance of evidence-based practice for the development of early years professional practice. Our major focus, therefore, will be practitioner research, how to do it and how it can support the development of practitioners and practice.

The wider project

The project is outlined as three action steps in Figure 3.1. Steps 1 and 2 each lasted four months and Step 3 took ten months. In meeting the three aims we outlined in the previous section we focused on the three action steps. However, we also gathered additional information through interviews, repertory grid techniques and questionnaires. Evidence from these have informed the direction of the project and ultimately our own evaluations of the initiative.

Step 1 consisted of a series of workshops where we led sessions for the project team on children as learners in literacy and in mathematics, action research and parental involvement. In Step 2 participants built up

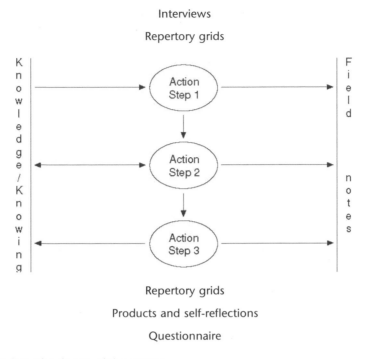

Figure 3.1 The design of the project

case studies of current practice on specific areas of provision in their own settings. In Step 3 they undertook action research curriculum and staff development projects with their colleagues in their settings. In both Steps 2 and 3 regular workshops were held to exchange information across settings and we visited each setting to give whatever help was needed. The project workshops were situated in each workplace setting in sequence, so that we could contextualize our discussions of each others' workplace practices, contexts and activities.

The participants were originally 20 pre-school practitioners from three local authorities, four local authority senior managers and the authors. The practitioners came from a range of professional backgrounds and settings. Backgrounds included teaching, social work and nursery nursing. Settings included daycare, pre-schools, schools, local authority special initiatives, childminding and a work-based childcare provision at a local hospital. The practitioners' names (pseudonyms) and individual project focuses are shown in Table 3.1 (four practitioners left the project because of moves or competing priorities). The practitioners were selected by their local authorities because of their ability to work with other professionals in order to share the outcomes of the initiative once it was completed. All

Table 3.1 The key practitioners and their projects

Practitioner	Project	Age range
Alison	Mathematics	(18–60 months)
Amy	Mathematics	(0–18 months)
Bernie	Mathematics	(36–60 months)
Frances	Music: literacy and mathematics	(18–36 months)
Gill	Mathematics	(0–36 months)
Ivy	Literacy	(0–18 months)
Jade	Mathematics	(36–60 months)
Jenny	Literacy	(0–18 months)
Josie	Mathematics	(18–60 months)
June	Mathematics	(0–18 months)
Meg	Literacy	(18–36 months)
Melissa	Mathematics	(36–60 months)
Millie	Mathematics	(0–18 months)
Molly	Literacy	(36–60 months)
Reza	Mathematics	(0–18 months)
Val	Literacy	(18–36 months)

three local authorities were therefore thinking carefully about how the benefits of the project could be sustained after its 18-month life.

The initial concerns and interests of the practitioners in the areas of literacy and numeracy were elicited through a short open-ended questionnaire given at a workshop at the start of Step 1. At this stage in the project we used the narrower term 'numeracy' to reflect government policy.

Their written responses revealed that there were some differences between concerns about coping with numeracy and with literacy. Participants appeared more confident in the area of literacy, how it was resourced and how parents might provide support. However, they did feel that they needed help with understanding the developmental sequences that underpin young children's acquisition of competence in literacy. Numeracy appeared to be relatively unexplored territory and this was particularly the case in relation to working with parents. The detailed responses also revealed the breadth of concerns which included catering with different age groups, bilingual children and the gendering of early education. Underlying these concerns was a sense that an emphasis on specific learning outcomes at the end of the pre-school experience might lead to the Key Stage 1 curriculum being filtered down to pre-schools. If this were to happen, it was feared that it would erode a number of firmly held professional beliefs about what constituted appropriate learning environments for very young children.

All the project participants were, therefore, united in the professional belief that if understandings of teaching and learning were to inform pre-school practice they had to be developed from the pockets of sound practice and expertise to be found among those already working with very young children. It was hoped, therefore that a strong sense of what an educationally oriented practice could be would develop through a sound mixing of the best of all the pre-school cultures found among the participants, helpfully flavoured by some research-based contributions from the authors. The blending of the mixture to create an understanding of practice depended entirely on the activities and contributions of the individual professionals and it is to these that we now turn.

Step 1: the workshops and readings

The contribution of the authors was most evident at Step 1. We ran workshops on literacy, numeracy, doing practitioner research and working with parents. We also produced digests of relevant research which were given to all the participants to help generate ideas for the individual projects that were to occur in the next two steps. Step 1 was also important as an opportunity to share current concerns and interpretations of those concerns, to visit each others' settings and to get a feel for where everyone was coming from as a practitioner and for people to learn to make their particular expertise explicit. The trust, openness and shared meanings that were built up slowly over the four months of Step 1 were, we would suggest, crucial to the success of the project.

Step 2: the case studies

In Step 2 the practitioners undertook small case studies in their own workplaces. We suggested case study as a starting point for the research for four reasons:

1. case study as a form of audit or analysis of current provision is an essential starting point for action research;
2. case study allows you to look at a complex aspect of practice or provision in a highly focused way;
3. small-scale case study is a manageable way of becoming familiar with methods of collecting data;
4. the material gathered in the case studies could be used as the starting point for discussions between participants at our monthly workshop sessions, allowing good ideas to be shared across settings.

So what is a case? We worked with social science understandings of case and case study. Here a case is usually described as a 'unit of analysis'. It can be, for example, a family, a work team, an area of a pre-school setting, a child, an aspect of the curriculum. Cases are therefore seen to consist of sets of complex relationships that can be observed within a fairly distinct boundary. Yet, at the same time, cases also interact with the context in which they are situated so the boundaries are permeable.

You will remember from our discussion of Bronfenbrenner's (1979) work in Chapter 1 that we were able to understand 'the child as learner' by locating her or him in relation to his or her family, the social policies that influenced the patterns of family life and the political priorities that led to those social policies. Cases therefore provide distinct focuses for us as researchers, but can also be connected to events outside the case. In our project the cases were aspects of the curriculum, specific areas in the work settings or sets of relationships between parents and professionals. These cases were located within the efforts of local pre-school providers to get to grips in 1997 with the curricular and professional development demands of *Desirable Outcomes* (DfEE/SCAA 1996).

Cases can be used in a number of ways in research (see Stake 1994; Edwards and Talbot 1999; Edwards 2001). In Step 2 of our project we wanted cases to be descriptions of what was going on so that they could be used as stimuli for discussions between the key practitioners and also between them and their immediate colleagues when the time came for planning Step 3. We also knew that once professionals start to look in a focused way at aspects of their own provision they see them afresh and any number of professional issues arise when thinking about what has been seen. Our research partners therefore started their case studies wanting to answer the question *what is going on here?* In the project we focused on practice which promoted children's learning. As we reflect eight years later, we are aware that a stronger focus on the ways in which the settings as organizations, with their own histories which encouraged or limited practice and learning, would have been a useful addition to the design of the study. We shall return to that point in Chapter 9.

The case study process

Each participant was advised to go through the following process:

- think about the provision in your setting;
- look at your development plan if you have one;
- identify one area where you feel strongly that provision could be improved;

- identify the precise aspect of provision on which you want to focus;
- negotiate with colleagues in the area you have identified to allow them to feel comfortable about being part of the case study;
- select the data collection method(s) you will need in order to find out what is happening;
- plan when you will be able to collect the data without disturbing the case;
- gather your evidence.

Gathering evidence in the case study

To ensure that the evidence that was gathered gave a valid picture of provision, we asked practitioners to design their case studies so that they used three methods of data collection and collected their material systematically over a period of time. In doing so we were working with the idea of *triangulation* which is central to robust case study work. Triangulation, as the term implies, means getting as strong a purchase on the case as is possible by approaching it from a number of angles. 'Strong' and 'as is possible' are important concepts in practitioner case study. Case studies do rely on rich evidence, but there comes a point where the over-zealous practitioner researcher can disrupt the case in the quest for evidence. We strongly advised practitioners to do only what was feasible. We were therefore keen to work with data collection methods that were fairly unobtrusive.

Research diaries were kept by everyone in the project. These were spiral bound hardback notebooks. They were used in the following way. Working from the front we used the left-hand pages to jot down observations of, for example, children at work in the construction area or notes made during or immediately after staff meetings or workshops, and we dated the notes. If the books were not at hand, jottings were made on the paper that was available and later clipped into the notebooks. The facing right-hand pages were left free to be used for immediate reflections on the notes or for later reflections once themes started to emerge or when someone at a workshop said something that helped to interpret what had been recorded. Working from the back of the notebooks we collected useful addresses, clipped in cuttings from professional journals or the press, or wrote references to books or papers we heard about in our discussions. The diaries then served as records of observations and developing interpretations of events and proved to be the most useful research tool for everyone concerned. In effect the diaries were like the working sketch books of designers and artists.

Photographs were used to produce time sequence observations. If a sense of an activity over a period of time was needed, for example to see how children made use of the materials available in an area of the pre-school, then photographs were taken at regular time intervals. For example, one photograph every 60 seconds for ten minutes would produce a time sequence of ten photographs. These proved to be very useful case study material for our purposes as the pictures provided the opportunity for considerable discussion both at workshops and in the settings between the practitioners there.

Video recordings can be particularly useful when trying to capture the detail of interactions or how children use particular resources, but are not always as useful as one might expect when trying to capture the more general flow of activities across a busy pre-school setting. Ivy, who worked with mothers to help them interact with their babies, gathered some very useful evidence using a video camera which allowed her to capture the gradual thawing of the mothers as they learnt to play with their children.

Written observations were made using a range of methods:

- narrative descriptions of key events were written and stored in the research diaries;
- specific observations of children using materials in settings were undertaken using the schedule we discuss in Chapter 8;
- the target child method of observation developed by Kathy Sylva and her team was used to track specific children or to observe how staff were interacting with children.

The target child method of observation (Sylva *et al.* 1980) is so useful and flexible that we shall describe it here (it can also be found in Edwards and Talbot 1999). The method as we used it in the case studies involved the following stages.

1. Identify a target to observe – for example, the target could be a child or a colleague – and select the setting for the observation – for example, the child in the water area.
2. Identify the time you will observe the target (you will need at least 15 minutes for a 10-minute observation and you should undertake more than one 10-minute observation of the target, though not necessarily on the same day).
3. Prepare a set of observation schedules. These consist of sheets of A4 paper each divided horizontally into five blocks and vertically into first a narrow column, followed by two columns of equal width (see Figure 3.2). One sheet of paper is used for five minutes of observation. When you use it you will write the time in the first column – for example, 10.01 against the first block, 10.02 against

the second etc. In each block in the second column you will write down everything that you see your target doing or saying in the course of one minute. You will keep the third column blank to be used for annotating your observations later. For ten minutes of observation you will need two sheets.

4. Find a place to observe where, if possible, you can hear as well as see your target.

5. Write down as quickly as possible what your target does. You will need an easy-to-read watch so that you know when to move on to the next minute block on the observation sheet. You will also need a shorthand system such as initials for names and arrows for actions.

6. After ten minutes, stop and take your observations to somewhere where you can have five minutes to tidy them so that they will make sense later. Use the reverse sides of the observation sheets to make any notes you wish about the event. For example, you might want to note what the colleague had said she had hoped to achieve, or why you were observing that particular child.

7. Repeat your observation at least once with the same target person in the same setting.

8. What you put in the third column will depend on the focus of your study. If, for example, you are interested in children's mark-making as Mollie was, then you will focus on what adult actions led to successful mark-making or to a child refusing to cooperate and you will begin to label them in the third column.

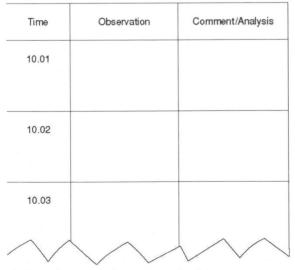

Figure 3.2 Part of a target observation schedule

Notes from staff meetings proved to be extremely useful. A number of participants started their data collection with 'mindstorms' with colleagues in which they listed, for example, how joining in the musical activities in the pre-school was already benefiting all the children, or what strengths parents had as educators of the children in their pre-school. Sometimes these notes provided very useful diagnostic material for planning just how fast or carefully it would be appropriate to work with colleagues at Step 3. Melissa, for example, through staff meeting discussions, was able to clarify her understanding of the extent to which her co-workers saw the educational potential in the number activities she was making available for children.

Other written material such as booklets for parents, curriculum plans or assessments of children were easily collected. Their relevance and currency was discussed at workshops and notes were made of the discussions in the research diaries.

Tape-recordings can be very helpful when focusing on children's language or interactions between children and adults. However, the noise levels in most pre-schools and the speed at which most young children move around meant that it was not always an attractive option. When tape-recordings of children's talk were successfully undertaken they were specifically set up by taking children to a quiet corner and recording them while they worked at an activity. Staff meetings were sometimes recorded, but it was often difficult to hear everyone and the recordings had to be listened to, which was time consuming.

Questionnaires and interviews can also be used in case studies. However we did not use them very much in our project, partly because they too can be very time consuming, are difficult to do well (particularly when researching your own setting) and produce a lot of data that take a long time to analyse. However, Meg drew usefully on information from a short questionnaire to parents about how much they wanted to be involved with her centre to gauge the pace at which she should work with parents. Reza and June used both interviews and questionnaires in their attempt to discover how much music was part of the lives and language development of the children in the multicultural nursery in which June worked. We did not recommend interviews as they can be intrusive and disrupt the case. However, if you would like to know more about interviews and questionnaires see Oppenheim (1992) or Edwards and Talbot (1999).

We found that short written observations, photographs and short written records of conversations made during observations to be the most useful pieces of evidence both in our discussions at workshops and when practitioners discussed what they had noticed with their immediate colleagues. This was because the written evidence could be photocopied and read and the photographs looked at by a group of people.

These observations therefore became public texts around which the expertise of everyone involved could be shared and developed. Insights from education colleagues about the educational potential in activities were useful to those with a care background, while those who worked in care settings drew on their understandings of attention to children's emotional state and the quality of adult–child interactions and contributed these. We were aiming at developing enriched understanding of practice and learning which were shared across the practitioner group. The case study discussions based on evidence from such a variety of settings were fertile starting points. The project seemed to operate as a sort of *boundary zone* between the different workplace settings where new ideas could be shared, developed and refined. In psychological terms, our coresearchers were developing more complex representations of children as learners and of the practices that might support that learning. One challenge, of course, was how those representations might be taken into practice and be refined further in practice. The solution was found in action research.

Step 3: the action research

Step 3 was the action research stage of the project. In this stage participants developed an aspect of practice in their settings, monitored the development and looked at its impact on the experiences of children. Importantly, they took the ideas (i.e. representations), that had been developed among the group in Steps 1 and 2 back into their own settings and integrated them into practice while helping their colleagues work with them too.

We used a simple model of action research which started with *review* and moved on to *planning*, which was then followed by *action*. The action was carefully *monitored* and then *reviewed* along with possibilities for further development which would enable the cycle to start again (see Figure 3.3).

Our case studies in Step 2 were our reviews. Conversations in the workshops and in the various pre-school settings about the case study data were the jumping-off points for planning the actions to be taken in Step 3. The conversations focused on how the situation described by the cases could be developed to bring out the educational potential in the activities. Ideas were shared and plans for curriculum development began to take shape. We were ready to plan our actions. At that point we had to get very practical and think about *feasibility* and *timescale*. There is always the danger that practitioner researchers can become so excited about the possibilities for development found in a case study that they try to do too much too quickly.

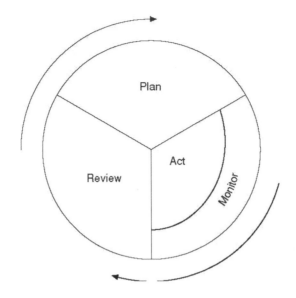

Figure 3.3 An action research cycle

Using timelines for planning

To deal with feasibility and timescale we used timelines to guide our planning. These proved to be important because they constantly reminded us of just how long change takes and how much care needs to be put into developing the confidence of colleagues as they work with new ideas. An outline timeline for planning the development of children's mark-making is shown in Figure 3.4.

In Figure 3.4 we see that four months between September and December were taken up with preparing for the involvement of everyone in trying out the new ideas in practice. The action occurred between January and April and time was set aside throughout that period for staff to regularly discuss the developments as they were occurring. The outcome was a set of curricular guidelines on mark-making that everyone had some part in producing.

The phases in this example were as follows:

1. discussing the case study findings with colleagues and introducing the ideas developed in conversations in Steps 1 and 2;
2. planning any changes to pre-school organization and noting resource needs;
3. ordering resources;
4. making changes to the area where mark-making will occur;

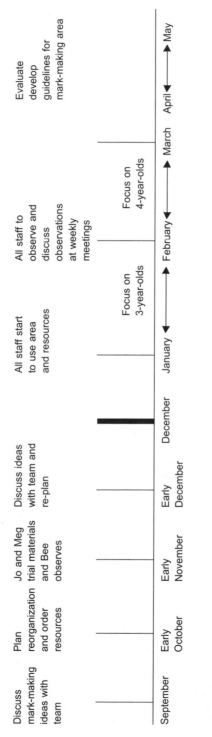

Figure 3.4 A Timeline for a piece of action research on mark-making in the construction area

5. trying out the ideas in a small way and monitoring the trial;
6. evaluating the trial of the new ideas;
7. adjusting ideas and re-planning;
8. agreeing how the actions will be monitored;
9. undertaking actions and monitoring the actions;
10. timetabling regular meetings to discuss what is being learnt about new strategies and the children;
11. adjusting strategies if necessary;
12. final evaluation and the development of curricular guidelines on mark-making.

Finding time to talk

In the project we used action research with two aims in mind. First we needed a way of allowing the expertise that existed among all the practitioners involved to be made explicit so that it could be shared and contribute to the knowledge base that informed practice. The knowledge that underpins expert practice is often referred to as tacit knowledge because it has become so much a part of the actions of expert practitioners that they simply don't need to think or talk about it. By asking practitioners to plan, monitor and evaluate aspects of practice, and to do that while drawing on some of the ideas we had shared about learning and curriculum, we were asking them to be explicit about their practice. As they talked they contributed their own meanings and interpretations to the developing discourse of and educationally oriented practice. Our second action research aim was that the systematic and public analysis of strategies to promote children's learning would mean that we could have some confidence in the reliability of the grounded curricular guidance the local authorities had been promised as an outcome of the project.

The need to talk about practice meant that our action research plans emphasized the opportunities for discussion within each setting, and between settings when the participants discussed progress at our monthly workshops. The need to undertake systematic analysis of actions meant that colleagues needed to work, as they did in the case studies, with non-intrusive but robust methods of data collection. Also, because we wanted to evaluate the effect of new ways of working, it was important that they collected evidence about what the children were able to do as a result of these innovations.

Monitoring the action

We used the same data collection methods that were suggested for case studies at Step 2 and found the diaries particularly useful as records of the story of each development. We added to these methods by attending particularly to collecting (i) examples of what the children did and (ii) feedback from parents. Evidence of what the children did included photographs of completed models or games; photographs showing how children were using resources – for example, measuring the boats they built out of big blocks or holding and enjoying books; their attempts at mark-making and emergent writing; and written observations which included their use of language and materials.

Feedback from parents was collected in two ways. Comments made by parents about their children and their new experiences were noted immediately in research diaries by almost everyone. For example, Millie and Amy noted the following comments about their songbook.

> I felt silly at first. But when I saw how Sarah responded I began to enjoy our singing sessions.

> I realize how OK it is to hold Joseph and sing to him. We both love these times together.

However, we also found that a great deal of evidence came from materials that were passed between pre-school settings and homes. The distressed mothers in Ivy's project were helped to build up brief profiles of their children and record their successes in interacting with them in games and songs at home. The mothers of the toddlers in Val's project made books which contained their child's photograph and information on what the child was doing which passed between the parents and Val. In both of these examples the books came to mean a great deal to the parents but also provided Ivy and Val with important evidence of the success of their projects. The parents in Josie's project on mathematics at home and in the nursery were eager to provide evidence of their children's work with number at home with, for example, photographs of children jumping down steps and counting them or proudly showing their sets of five nail varnishes laid out on a bed.

The evidence that was gathered during the monitoring of the planned actions was used, like the case study data, as shared texts and the basis of conversations about practice. We will see in Chapter 8 how staff in Alison's centre all used the same format for their observations of children as they worked as beginning mathematicians in the construction area and discussed what they observed at weekly meetings in ways that both shared what they had noticed about children and what they had learned about practice.

What we learnt from action research

What we learnt about how to support children as they experience mathematics and literacy-based activities in pre-school settings will be outlined in the next five chapters. At this point we shall focus on what the participants reported that they had learnt about themselves as practitioners and about their practice at the end of Step 3. First of all we shall look at their final reflections on their own experiences in the project at the end of Step 3 and then we shall draw on elements of a questionnaire completed four months after the project ended.

We asked each of the practitioners to write up their personal reflections on their experience of the project. In summary, action research seemed to serve a number of purposes. For Jenny it appeared to be a lifeline which kept her going while working alone on her project with babies and books. At the same time it fired her intellectual curiosity and helped her focus on the principles that lay behind the project. For Meg in her project on parental involvement in literacy and for Jade in her work with parents and everyday mathematics, the commitment to the project and the support of the group sustained them when other pressures took over. In Jade's case this included the need to evacuate the centre as a result of flooding which certainly meant adjustments to the timeline! For Melissa, involving colleagues in action research allowed her to start the curriculum developments she thought had long been necessary and allowed her to evaluate and adjust the developments as they were being implemented. For Molly, action research helped her rethink how she could best support the professional development of her staff and how important it was to help them see for themselves what needed to be done. For Alison, the project provided the focus for an energetic and enthusiastic staff team, and for Frances it was the opportunity to try out in a systematic way her own theories about how children gain from being in a musical environment. The common feature in all the reports was how much each of the participants felt they had learnt while trialling their ideas as action research and how much had been gained from being part of a group both at the level of the wider project and in their own settings.

Questionnaire evidence gathered from open-ended questions in the questionnaire distributed four months after the end of Step 3 revealed, for example, how much more aware colleagues were of the strengths that children bring with them to their pre-school settings and how they could use the particular strengths of parents to help their children develop as learners. The questionnaire data, in summary, revealed an increased confidence in being able to work flexibly and interactively with children as learners. This broad analysis is supported by the evidence gathered using repertory grids which we shall discuss in the next section.

Earlier in our discussion of action research we identified two aims for the action research phase of the project. These were (i) to help make explicit the tacit expertise of the participating practitioners so that it could be shared and contribute to their professional knowledge base and (ii) the systematic analysis in practice of the curricular guidance we were jointly developing. Our aims were very much in line with those suggested by John Elliott for action research. Writing about action research and teachers he suggests: 'Teachers may be unaware of their actions and of the beliefs and assumptions (theories) that underpin them. Understanding comes through the analysis of evidence about practice and the generation of new knowledge via the formulation and testing of action hypotheses in the light of such analyses' (Elliott 1994: 137).

Action research is clearly a powerful way of generating, using and evaluating the practical knowledge that was being developed. We also agree with Elliott's claim (Elliott 1994: 137) that action research can bring together 'the processes of pedagogical transformation and theory generation'. Our practitioner partners transformed aspects of their own practices at the same time as developing practical knowledge that they could share with others. We would, however, stress that the practical knowledge that was produced is itself contestable. That is, practical knowledge should be consistently scrutinized by a well-informed profession and not become ritualized in empty practices.

Developing informed confidence through research into practice

The project required practitioners to make important changes in their practices in order to provide the children with their educational entitlements and to research those changes so that they could share their experiences with other practitioners. The practitioners who were involved clearly felt it was a worthwhile experience. But we also had other evidence.

The research design provided in Figure 3.1 shows that we started the project by interviewing participants. We chose our interview sample of six participants to enable us to get views about current and future provision from experienced practitioners from the range of backgrounds and settings that was found across the project. We then used the material we gathered in the interviews to structure a more detailed data-gathering exercise using repertory grids. Repertory grid methodology is a sound and efficient way of revealing how people make sense of their immediate world (for further reading on repertory grids see Fransella and Bannister 1977 or Fransella and Thomas 1988).

We used a grid that would enable us to find out how participants were feeling and thinking in eight specific situations such as doing a puzzle with a child or talking to an inspector. Having decided on the situations we then used our interview material to provide us with statements about how practitioners might be making sense of each situation. These statements are called *constructs* in repertory grid methodology. Constructs are often likened to the blinkers through which we make sense of our experiences. For example, when we meet something new to us we categorize it using constructs. Constructs are bipolar, which means that a construct is a dimension with opposite feelings at each end. If whether people are gentle or aggressive is important to us we will place people we meet somewhere on the construct 'gentle–aggressive'. So when we meet someone new we might use a construct that has gentle and aggressive as its two poles to judge the extent to which the newcomer is gentle or aggressive. Our constructs are also personal and based on our own previous experiences, so gentle–aggressive may not be a construct used by everyone. Indeed, others may be judging the same newcomer as either aggressive or a wimp and hoping that she or he is aggressive.

We therefore had to be careful to select constructs that would make sense to most of the participants, that would help us measure the changes we wanted to measure and could be used when thinking about how as a professional one might think and feel in a particular situation. In Table 3.2 you can see the constructs that were finally selected and in Table 3.3 we have listed the situations.

The participants completed the grids individually by being talked into each situation by one of the authors and were then asked whether, for example, they felt confident in what they were saying or thought that there might be gaps in what they were saying. Participants were asked to respond on a five-point rating scale. So if they felt very confident while doing a puzzle they would record a rating of five, or if they felt that there were at least some gaps while talking to an inspector they would record two or three for that situation.

The grids were completed early in Step 1 and at the end of Step 3. We were therefore able to assess the impact of the project on the participants' thoughts and feelings about quite specific aspects of practice. In Table 3.2 we have given average ratings and the ranking for each construct and in Table 3.3 the average ratings and the rankings for each situation in both stages of the project. We selected the constructs so that a high rating would represent professional confidence.

Table 3.2 Rankings of importance of constructs before and after undertaking research

	At the start of Step 1		At the end of Step 3	
	Average rating	Rank	Average rating	Rank
Feel confident about what you say/think there may important gaps in what you are saying	3.7	1	4.6	1
Feel confident that your colleagues would say the same/have doubts that your colleagues would say the same	3.1	5	3.9	6
Know exactly what you want a particular child to learn/have quite general learning intentions in mind	3.2	3	4.2	3
Have the resources you need available/lack the resources you need	3.1	5	3.9	6
Think you are getting somewhere/feel frustrated	3.1	5	3.9	6
Think you can focus at the curriculum/have a number of competing concerns	3.0	7	4.0	4
Feel happy about the curriculm emphasis/ feel a sense of loss with the emphasis on the curriculum	3.4	2	4.4	2

Maximum rating = 5
Number of responses at the start of Step 1= 12
Number of responses at the end of Step 3 = 13

But we do recognize that, for example, having competing concerns is not necessarily a professional weakness in the complex world of early education.

In Table 3.2 we see very little difference in the ranking of importance of each construct at the start of Step 1 and the end of Step 3. Indeed there is also very little difference between each rating at the time of assessment. However, there are important differences between the average ratings at the start of Step 1 and the end of Step 3. The average ratings on each construct are considerably higher at the end of Step 3 in each case. We suggest that this increase demonstrates an increase in

Table 3.3 Ranking in feelings about situations before and after undertaking research

	At the start of Step 1		At the end of Step 3	
	Average rating	Rank	Average rating	Rank
Doing a puzzle with a 3-year-old who is a quick learner	3.7	1	4.0	6
Water play with a 3-year-old with delayed language development	3.2	5	3.9	7
Explaining to a new colleague how work in your nursery helps children to become literate	3.0	7.5	4.2	3
Explaining to a new colleague how work in your nursery helps a child to become numerate	3.0	7.5	4.2	3
Talking to a parent about how she or he can help her or his 3-year-old to start to read	3.3	3	3.7	8
Planning the literacy curriculum with colleagues	3.3	3	4.2	3
Planning the numeracy curriculum with colleagues	3.1	6	4.1	5
Explaining to an inspector how the environment has been created to support Children's learning	3.3	3	4.3	1

Maximum rating = 5
Number of responses at the start of Step 1 = 12
Number of responses at the end of Step 3 = 13

informed confidence among the participants over the period of the project. More specifically of particular interest in relation to the project aims are:

- satisfaction with the curricular emphases manifested in the project;
- satisfaction with resources suggesting that the educational potential of existing resources was being recognized;

- recognition that colleagues were also learning;
- the outstandingly high rating given to participants' own knowledge base.

When we turn to Table 3.3 we, of course, see a similar increase in average ratings between the start of Step 1 and the end of Step 3, but we also see changes in the rankings related to situations. These changes are important because they tell us where participants felt most informed and confident at the start of the project and again at the end. The pattern shown in Table 3.3 shows us that at the end of the project:

- participants were far more confident about explaining numeracy and literacy to new colleagues and about explaining to an inspector about how the nursery supported children's learning;
- the more traditional aspects of nursery provision (i.e. doing puzzles and talking to parents) showed slight increases in scores but were overtaken by more curriculum-related matters;
- as we might have predicted from our diagnoses at the outset of the project, colleagues were slightly more confident when planning the literacy curriculum than the numeracy curriculum.

These results are exciting because they show that a great deal of learning had occurred and that participants were demonstrating that learning in the way they thought about their everyday practices. Our sample is small and the project quite specific but we would suggest that the experience of evidence-based practice we monitored and supported did have a highly positive impact on the professional development of participants.

Inquiring professionals

We shall discuss the contexts of professional development in Chapter 9. Here we simply start to alert you to what our data told us about the importance of collaborative action research as a way of developing new professional identities. By professional identity we mean *a way of being, seeing and responding* while working professionally. We would expect an early years professional to work responsively and with flexibility and, for example, see the mathematics in a piece of striped material or wrapping paper and help a child to also see some of the mathematics available there.

We were, therefore, particularly excited by the repertory grid data which suggested that our research partners were seeing increased educational potential in existing resources. Our field notes at workshops in Steps 2 and 3 had indicated that colleagues were thinking and acting with increasingly educational insights as they worked with familiar materials. The repertory grid data seemed to confirm these indications and suggested that a new professional culture of early education was being developed in which existing materials were given new meanings as they were being used in new and more informed ways.

These findings are very much in line with work on professional cultures and how participants in a culture learn to use the materials and the language associated with cultural activity in increasingly informed and culturally accepted ways (Lave and Wenger 1991; Cole 1996; Cole *et al.* 1997). Professional cultures and sociocultural psychology are complex fields of study, but there are lessons to be learnt from them when considering early education as a developing form of professional practice. Much of the work in this field considers how learners are guided into being active members of existing cultures. In our study we were looking at how a new form of professional culture was being developed in action, and sociocultural psychology provided a useful set of lenses through which to observe aspects of the action that took place.

For example, sociocultural psychology helped us to see how a new form of professional culture was taking shape in our project through evidence-based discussions of developing professional practices. James Wertsch, writing about cultural memories, reminds us of the extent to which we build up a sense of ourselves as a community through the language we use when we recall aspects of the community and recount its stories (Wertsch 1997). Action research, with its emphasis on public discussion of the narratives of practice, is illuminated by Wertsch's analysis. In our study, discussions of what was happening in pre-school settings were informed by the research-based knowledge provided by the authors and by the current research of the settings-based participants. These discussions proved to be useful vehicles for meaning sharing.

Suggested reading

Penn, H. (1999) *Theory, Policy and Practice in Early Childhood Services* (Buckingham: Open University Press) is an edited international collection of papers which theorize the policy and practice developments in early childhood services. The chapter by Anne Edwards draws on the study discussed here and attempts to answer the question 'Research and practice: is there a dialogue?'

An excellent guide to the practicalities of action research is Hopkins, D. (1993) *A Teachers' Guide to Classroom Research*, 2nd edn (Buckingham:

Open University Press). You should not be deterred by the title, as the ideas discussed transfer very easily to pre-school settings.

Action research and case study are also strands in a practical guide to practitioner research which is sensitive to the demands of workplace research: Edwards, A. and Talbot, R. (1999) *The Hardpressed Researcher: A Research Handbook for Education, Health and Social Care* (London: Longman).

MacNaughton, Rolfe & Siraj-Blatchford (eds) (2001) *Doing Early Childhood Research: Theory and Process. An International Perspective* (Buckingham: Open University Press) is an excellent comprehensive guide to doing research in the pre-school phase.

4 Young children as learners

The what, who and how of learning

Decisions about curricula for young children are often gambles. We simply can't predict exactly what knowledge and kinds of expertise will be needed 20 years from now. However, we can be pretty certain that the very young children of today need to become adults who are able to adapt to work practices that will change throughout their working lives and able to cope with the changing demands coming from families and communities. Those of us who are involved in the education of young children therefore need to focus on helping children to become resilient learners, to enjoy learning and to feel that they are people who are able to learn. This is no small challenge but it is a safe bet that investment in children's dispositions to learn will pay dividends.

This point is made clearly by Schweinhart and Weikart (1993: 4) when they discuss the lasting change that occurred as a result of High Scope interventions with disadvantaged children in the USA in the 1970s:

> The essential process connecting early childhood experience to patterns of improved success in school and community seemed to be the development of habits, traits and dispositions that allowed the child to interact positively with other people and with tasks. This process was based neither on permanently improved intellectual performance nor on academic knowledge.

Schweinhart and Weikart are pointing to dispositions. We can see dispositions as orientations towards the world around us. We therefore need to support children's orientations or dispositions so that they approach activities in ways that allow them to be open to the learning opportunities to be found in them. Schweinhart and Weikart's emphasis is on helping children to see themselves as people who can learn. Their focus is on creating learners. An emphasis on disposition was also central to New Zealand early years curriculum (MoE 1993) where they referred to dispositions as 'habits of mind' and 'patterns of learning' which provide the foundation for future independent learning.

We know that these habits of mind are shaped in young children's interactions with others and in the opportunities for being a learner that are available to them, particularly in their families and in early childhood settings. We can think about dispositions as learnt competences and within-person characteristics that orient behaviour. It seems that is the view taken by Schweinhart and Weikart. However, seeing disposition as only within the child does not explain how a child may be oriented to think and act as a competent mathematical thinker in one setting but not in another. Therefore it may help to think about dispositions as within person propensities which are brought into play when they are supported by the situation. These pathways, the opportunities for participation or action, and dispositions to engage may vary between settings.

One advantage of that view is that it allows us to see how important it is to strive for some alignment between the support children receive in early childhood education and the other settings in which they are able to learn. This is an argument for multi-professional collaboration and for strong reciprocal links between home and early education settings. These collaborations can help children to be seen as learners in all settings so that dispositions to engage are supported across settings.

Focusing on pathways of participation does not mean that we can overlook *what* is being learnt. Participation is not only about behaviour. It involves developing an increasingly rich set of concepts to be used when we try to make sense of the world, and it highlights children's use of the concepts that they encounter in these socially sustained pathways. Early educators therefore have a difficult task. They need to attend to *what* children are learning, how they become people *who* are learners and *how* children learn and *how* that learning is supported.

Traditionally, early education has been based on a developmental view of how children learn. Important as this is, recent thinking about learning suggests that the *what, who* and *hows* of learning are crucially interlinked. For example, a disposition to seek out the patterns in a striped shirt is nurtured by previous success as a mathematical thinker. This success is, in turn, connected to a developing capacity to deal with mathematical concepts and the ways that the setting is oriented to mathematical actions, through the resources available and the actions of adults and other learners.

The early years practitioners in our partnership confirmed this analysis of the interrelatedness of all three aspects of learning. In their own learning they moved rapidly from seeing, for example, mark-making as a curriculum area to be covered, to concentrating on creating contexts in which children became meaningful mark-makers, where resources were available and adults supported and challenged them.

The project became increasingly focused on how children's learning was supported in the experiences provided in the different settings. Therefore we began to frame these experiences with a sociocultural view of learning that allowed us to take into account the *what, who* and *hows* of children's learning and that helped us to plan future developments. The approach offers a focus on learners, how they are assisted in their sense-making, and the cultural messages in the contexts in which they learn. It also asks us to move to and fro between thinking about individual learners and about the cultural context that surrounds, shapes and permeates their thinking and action. So, for example, we can see dispositions both as learnt, within-child attributes and as externally supported possibilities for action.

A sociocultural view of learning: learning and context

There has been a lot written about sociocultural approaches to learning which focuses on participation as behaviour and underplays Vygotsky's original emphasis on learning as a change in how a child understands and acts. One of the major contributions of Vygotsky, the forefather of sociocultural approaches, was to help us see that how we think is revealed in how we use material and conceptual tools. He was interested in behaviour, but only to the extent that it revealed how we think so that he could then work on enhancing that thinking.

A quick example. If a 4-year-old is doing a jigsaw puzzle she may approach it randomly, or she may look at the picture on the box and start to sort pieces by colour, or she may identify the flat-sided pieces and start to build the frame. What she does reveals the concepts she is bringing into play as she completes the puzzle. She will, of course, have learnt those concepts while doing puzzles with others who know how to approach them and who shared that knowledge with her in their actions and language. She will have learnt a lot in those interactions. As well as how to set about doing a puzzle she will have learnt persistence, the care of resources, that puzzles are a worthwhile activity and that working with others involves sensitivity and turn-taking.

Because they are concerned, at least in part, with thinking and the use of knowledge, sociocultural approaches do have aspects in common with Piagetian ideas about learning. They acknowledge that learning occurs as a result of active involvement with the environment; and that children construct, that is build up, increasingly complex under-standings over time. So it is likely that very young children will operate, at times, with misconceptions about the world. However, sociocultural approaches are more clearly rooted in analyses of culture and context. They tell us that children learn what is important in their culture through interactions in and with that culture. They focus on how language carries the meanings and values of a particular culture. Also they remind us how opportunities for learning can vary from setting to setting.

Let us, therefore, look at just four of the key features of a sociocultural approach to understanding learning and how we found them useful in the project. The four key features are:

1. the impact of cultural expectations (i.e. we learn to do what we think the context demands of us);
2. the relationship between our sense of who we are and what we do (i.e. between our identities, dispositions and our actions);
3. an understanding that learning occurs through interaction with others (i.e. through language and imitation);
4. an understanding that learning occurs through and in the use of resources that are valued in our cultures (i.e. through using resources in the same way as others do).

Cultural expectations

Sociocultural psychology tells us that learning is a process of being able to participate increasingly effectively in the world in which we find ourselves. At birth, that world is fairly straightforward, albeit heavily emotionally charged, consisting of the presence or absence of sources of food and comfort. It soon becomes more complicated so that, for example, young children learn that although rowdy behaviour might be fine in the garden it is not appropriate in the supermarket.

By the time children are ready to enter compulsory schooling it is usually expected that they know how to participate as pupils, rather than members of a family, when at school. There is also the expectation that they have begun to acquire particular ways of thinking, such as how to be someone who can solve a puzzle or handle a book. These expectations are, of course, more likely to be fulfilled by children from some backgrounds than from others, simply because different families will provide different pathways of participation with different resources and opportunities for sense-making, with the result that different cultural expectations will have started to shape children's thinking.

These are important ideas for early educators. They help us understand two important issues. First, children who arrive at early education settings from different cultural backgrounds are likely to bring different ways of making sense and engaging. It is therefore necessary to try to understand what these are and to value them as important and valued prior learning. Second, they remind practitioners of how complex, yet crucial, the learning environment is and how it is worth investing time in thinking about and constructing it. The environment is an intricate interaction of spaces, resources, values, patterns of expected behaviour and interactions. These are under the control of early educators and can be shaped and sustained by them.

In summary, sense-making and action are heavily dependent on what is possible and expected. Learners look for cues in contexts for guidance on how to interpret what is going on and how to respond to those interpretations. Educators who can move between thinking about learners and thinking about how their learning experiences are shaped have a powerful approach to pedagogy. They need, of course, to identify first the kinds of thinking they want to develop. Siraj-Blatchford and Sylva (2004) describe this kind of analyses done by practitioners as 'pedagogical framing'. That is 'the behind the scenes aspects of pedagogy which include planning, resources and establishment of routines'. They suggest the settings that are most effective at enhancing children's development offer both pedagogical framing and interactions oriented to developing children's thinking and learning.

The way that Alison shaped the construction area in her pre-school centre is a nice example of pedagogical framing.

> Alison wanted to provide 3- and 4-year-old children with opportunities to think and act as young designers and mathematicians with construction materials. Having re-sourced the area with books about boats, small- and medium-size wooden blocks, yellow 'engineers'' helmets, tape mea-sures, paper and pencils, staff encouraged children to work in pairs to build boats. Once finished, the boats were measured and the measurements recorded by the children. The children were encouraged to operate as designers and mathematicians and to participate in a sequence of actions from planning to recording. The children tackled the activities in ways that reflected their own physical development and grasp of concepts and achieved a sense of success through completing the activities. They therefore left the construction area with memories of an experience in which thinking and acting as designers and mathematicians was associated with their own effectiveness.

Interestingly, the practitioners behaved in a range of ways in and around the construction area. Sometimes they would use a child's long-term involvement in an activity as an opportunity for a detailed observation which they would then discuss with colleagues. Sometimes they would interact to increase the cognitive challenge the activity in the way currently associated with 'excellent' provision identified by Siraj-Blatchford and Sylva (2004). At other times they would leave the children to work together while they worked intensively with another group, confident that the options available to the children in the construction area would support their learning and structure their engagement.

Identities and dispositions

One way of looking at disposition so that we can become clearer about how adults can support children's dispositions to respond positively and appropriately, is to connect disposition to children's developing sense of who they are and what they can do. To make the connection we need to look briefly at the idea of 'personal identity' – that is, the *who* of learning. Rom Harré, for example, uses the words 'self' and 'identity' inter-changeably and talks of both as organizing principles for action (Harré 1983).

Harré's definition helps us to see that our sense of who we are – which will include what we are capable of doing – guides our orientation to the world around us and ultimately how we participate in it. For example, if a child's identity includes a belief that she is good with numbers, she will find herself attracted to number activities. At a more detailed level, if that identity includes a capacity to see mathematics as sets of patterns then the child will seek out the patterns in the learning opportunities provided. In other words, she will have a disposition to engage with aspects of the mathematics available in the experience provided for her.

The children in Alison's construction area were, through their role play, developing dispositions to design and evaluate as part of the construction process. They were able to operate at levels that reflected their capabilities and their successes were supported and recognized by the adults.

Dispositions are rooted in our sense of our likely effectiveness. The challenge for educators is to assist the development of a sense of effectiveness through careful and sensitive support while children acquire the capabilities and understandings which will underpin their effectiveness. Here we connect the *how* and the *what* to the *who* of learning and need to examine the relationships that support early learning. Claxton and Carr (2004) offer some guidelines for thinking about how adults can enhance children's dispositions in early education settings. Reminding us that a disposition is not acquired, rather that we are disposed towards certain ways of acting, they look at how dispositions are supported by the environments created by practitioners. They suggest that adults should at the very least create environments that are 'affording' i.e. provide opportunities for children's active engagement. Better still is an 'inviting' environment which highlights clearly what is valued and gives some guidance to the child. Best of all is what they call a 'potentiating' context, which stretches and develops young children. They argue that potentiating environments involve frequent participation in shared activity.

Learning often occurs in interaction with others

The learning trajectory followed by most children from birth to 5 can be summarized as a gradual and parallel shift from interdependence to a capacity for independence and from a focus on personal sense-making to a focus on public meanings. Hence, the role of carers of young children is to support them as they acquire the capacity to participate in their social worlds.

Their responsibilities shift from the close and often symbiotic (mutually interdependent) relationships of key caregivers with infants immediately after birth and through much of the first year of life, to supporting children as they begin to experience and act upon a world that is external to their relationship with their caregivers. Finally the role becomes one of assisting children to understand the external world in the way that it is understood by other members of society.

Let us look at these three stages in turn and consider their implications for supporting children as learners. Although we are presenting them as a set of stages we are not proposing a simple continuum. We very much agree with, for example, Goldstein, (1999) and van Oers and Hännikäinen (2001) that caring, reciprocal relationships are central to the co-construction of mind and that this is markedly so throughout the early years of life. Adults will therefore find themselves, for example, working intersubjectively with 5-year-olds if that is what is needed.

The intersubjective phase

Initially children experience the world, and participate in it, through their relationships with their main caregivers who bring them into involvement with some of the basic features of social life by highlighting particular behaviours. The most important of these behaviours is the turn-taking that underpins, for example, language development. Young babies are not, however, entirely passive participants in these relationships.

Colwyn Trevarthen's detailed analyses of videotaped interactions between mothers and babies in their first few months of life (see Trevarthen 1977 for an introduction to his work) has drawn attention to the finely tuned patterns of interaction that occur. It has shown the extent to which these interactions can be mutual and not simply a matter of infants responding to their mothers. Trevarthen describes this turn-taking and synchronizing of responses as *co-regulation* (Trevarthen 1993). Importantly, co-regulation seems to happen as part of interactions in which mothers adapt their behaviour to the rhythms of their children and allow them to appear to be taking the lead so that a conversation-like interaction (or *protoconversation*) occurs.

The close relationship between infant and caregiver which Trevarthen observed and which enables an infant to experience the world in the physical and emotional safety provided by the relationship is characterized by *intersubjectivity*. Intersubjectivity was first described as the *meshing* that occurs between infant and caregiver which allows an infant to be inducted into understandings of what is important in the caregiver's culture (Newson and Newson 1975). It is often described in studies of infancy as a *meeting of minds*, where one of the minds is already steeped in the culture and where the other is being brought into the culture.

Intersubjectivity therefore demands considerable attention to the emotional state of infants and a capacity to slow down and tune into young children's ways of experiencing the world so that children are brought into interaction with the world. One of the most important elements of intersubjective relationships is how they help infants to develop as members of society with their own intentions and capabilities. A key feature of the adult role in an intersubjective relationship, in the Western world, appears to be to act *as if* the infant has intentions and is able to make evaluations. We see this behaviour in the conversations that mothers have with infants about feeding – for example, 'You want your bottle now don't you, I can tell'. This *as if* behaviour appears to prepare children for their later intentional and purposeful interactions with the world.

What we know of intersubjectivity is reason enough, we would argue, for ensuring that key worker systems are safeguarded, particularly for infants. If education is to be a feature of provision from birth we need to attend carefully to the subtle and demanding nature of work with babies. In our research partnership understandings of intersubjectivity fed two quite different projects.

Millie and Amy in their inner-city nursery worked cautiously and carefully in this area through the use of 'action songs'. They collected songs from the nursery workers and the parents involved in the nursery. They then produced a song book with, alongside each song, suggestions for ways of holding the babies and for actions associated with the lyrics. The songs were sung both at home and at the nursery. In both settings the infants were held in similar ways and were involved in consistent sets of patterns and responses with both sets of caregivers.

Millie and Amy's work also connected with another important feature of relationships between children and their caregivers in the first year of life: the involvement of children in *language formats* (Bruner 1983). Language formats are usually described as the frequently routine language repetitions associated with, for example, bath or mealtimes, or found in action songs. Bruner argued that these formats help children to understand that conversations involve interactions and that there is order to language. Therefore language formats provide children with important pre-linguistic skills.

Ivy's work with intersubjectivity was, however, quite different and involved her in therapeutic work with distressed parents. She worked in collaboration with speech therapists in her project with mothers who were experiencing problems in interacting with their babies as a result of depression. These mothers and their children quite clearly had not experienced intersubjective meshing and the children were not inter-acting appropriately with others in the nursery as a result. Ivy role-modelled interactions with the children which involved eye contact, sustained interactions through the language formats of repetition games and ways of responding to the children's overtures such as their smiles, offerings of objects etc. In the informal setting, where Ivy would sit on the floor alongside the older children, mothers were encouraged to watch and to respond when they felt ready to do so. Although attendance was often spasmodic, video evidence shows how mothers learnt to respond to their children and to sustain several turns of interaction with them.

Ivy's project was a strong example of how our mainly curriculum project overlapped at times with more fundamental issues of building a capacity for reciprocity and the development of young children's resilience through sound relationships with their primary caregivers. It was a good example of both interagency collaboration and the involvement of parents to support the learning pathways of these vulnerable children.

Learning to look outwards

Once infants have gained some sense of their own intentionality through knowing that adults will respond to them and they are familiar with turn-taking, they are ready to look beyond the familiar patterns of sense-making found in their intersubjective relationships. This is an important stage in the move towards being able to deal with the social world and the public meanings found in it.

The key concept here is a *joint involvement episode* (JIE) (Schaffer 1992). In a JIE an adult and a child pay joint attention to, and act together on, an object. An object may be a toy, part of the environment or a task such as making a 'pie'. As children get older the object may be a play on words or a joke. The important point is that JIEs direct children's attention to objects and events outside their relationships with their caregivers while giving them opportunities to act on these objects within the security and fund of expertise available in their caregiver relationships.

Schaffer therefore emphasizes that adults in JIEs should be sensitive to children's needs and abilities so that children are able to try out their ability to communicate with others while receiving the kind of support that assists them to develop as communicators. There is now considerable evidence to connect experience of JIEs with language development. Gordon Wells, in his study of children's language at home found a strong and positive relationship between the rate of language development at 30 months and the proportion of speech directed by the mother to the child during shared activities such as joint book-reading, play or sharing household chores (Wells 1987).

The Effective Provision of Pre-school Education (EPPE) study (Sylva *et al.* 2004) has more recently highlighted the importance of what they call 'sustained shared thinking' for children from 3 to 5. One element of the study examined in detail the practice of 28 practitioners from 12 preschool settings identified as effective in relation to child development outcomes. They found that child-initiated interactions between children and adults, which were extended by adults who increased the challenge for the child and 'lifted the level of thinking', were more likely to be found in settings where children made the most developmental progress (Siraj-Blatchford and Sylva 2004).

As we discussed JIEs during our workshops and related them to activities in various pre-school settings we saw them as extensions, or the next phase on, from the sound meshing that occurred in intersubjective interactions with infants. It was clear, for example, from Ivy's project that JIEs could not occur before the children had experienced the support that came from intersubjective relationships with primary caregivers. During our workshop discussions of evidence from the projects we gave both intersubjective meshing and JIEs the label of 'good one-to-ones' and were particularly excited by the way JIEs provided a framework for understanding the role of adults in interactions around objects with children from their second year of life. Jenny's project with babies and books, which aimed at encouraging mothers to interact with their babies and toddlers as they shared books, illustrates the continuum of 'good one-to-ones' that was a feature of several of the projects.

Working independently (with just a little help)

This phase marks a shift to children's independent action and use of public meanings when they communicate with others in the pre-school years. It is frequently the most difficult for adults to manage as it requires them to maintain sensitivity to children's need for support together with an ability to intervene without inhibiting children's sense-making in context. In the previous two stages, adults have provided a supporting structure for children's thinking and actions as part of their close relationships with children. Now the support has increasingly to occur outside relationships that have dependency at their core. We therefore need to look carefully at how adults provide support, or *scaffolding*, at this stage of children's development as learners.

Scaffolding has been defined as 'the contingent control of learning' by an adult with a child (Wood 1986). It is worth noting that the term was never used by Vygotsky. David Wood's definition is important because the word 'contingent' reminds us that scaffolding as a form of support needs to be sensitively responsive to (that is, contingent upon) the learner's need for assistance. The responsive nature of support is particularly relevant when working with very young learners who are gaining confidence as effective participants in the world and are developing dispositions to engage with the learning opportunities provided.

All too often, when scaffolding is discussed in the context of compulsory schooling and class teaching, it becomes simplified into a format for lesson planning where children are expected to work increasingly independently over the course of a lesson. Scaffolding learning is, however, a much more interactive process and demands close observation and continuous assessment of children as they participate in the learning contexts provided for them. In some ways scaffolding can be seen as a form of *guided participation*. Guided participation is, however not simply based on interactions between adults and children. Children's participation in an activity is also, in part, shaped by the resources available and the expectations for the use of the resources in a particular setting.

While Vygotsky did not use the term 'scaffolding' he did work with the idea of the *zone of proximal development* (ZPD). Like scaffolding, this concept has become over-simplified over the years, so that is often teamed with scaffolding and presented as an instrumental process of leading a child from what she knows to what she needs to know. It is worth returning to how Vygotsky tried to develop the concept of the ZPD as it reminds us of the extent to which development is interwoven with what he referred to as the *social situation of development.* He began, shortly before he died, to see the *leading activity* as the main source of development. The idea of a strong relationship between leading activity and development, which is teased out in some detail in Chaiklin (2004), became central to Vygotsky's focus on how the cultural is incorporated into mind and action. Chaiklin suggests that 'The notion of "leading activity" is a way to identify the particular relations in the social situation of development that are likely to contribute to the development of functions that lead to the structural reorganization of a child's psychological functions' (p. 47). Importantly, leading activities are culturally and historically constructed so that the social situation of development which will shape the minds of, for example, 2-year-olds will vary across cultures. Early education is a leading activity in its own right and should be constructed so that it contains opportunities for the development of thinking and action.

The children in Alison's construction area were guided into specific ways of participating as engineers, builders and mathematicians. Practitioners selected the materials available to them (for example, the sizes of the blocks available, tape measures, role play clothing and paper for recording); brought resources to their attention and encouraged them to plan, complete, measure and record. The following is an example of the kinds of learning promoting interactions that occurred in Alison's construction area.

The area this time was designed to engage children in working with shapes and the adult was undertaking a focused observation of the child. (The child was 4 years and 6 months.)

The child (C) takes out a shape book and turns to a page with a house on it. Sally, the adult (A), sits down and watches (C).

C: I want to make a house. (*Gets out large wooden bricks. Turns to adult.*) How do I do it Sally?

A: Look in the picture book, there's a triangle box at the top and a square shape for the house with straight lines.

C: (*Picks up two wedge bricks and places them on floor. Glances at the book and points at the top of the house. Places a rectangle brick in front of the two wedges.*) I don't know what comes next Sally.

A: Right, tell me about this so far then.

C: It's the roof.

A: Right. Then we need the long straight lines to make the side of the house.

C: (*Looks at the bricks and selects a long rectangle. Places it at right angles to the roof on the left side and repeats for the right side. Looks at A, and A nods in response.*) Which one?

A: (*Points to the house in the book.*) The small rectangle for the bottom of the house.

C: (*Picks up brick.*) This one?

A: (*Shakes head.*) Look at the shape. Is it the same as this? (*Points at the book.*)

C: No … erm … what is it then?

A: Well, have a think. Tell me what you think it is.

C: Don't know. (*Looks at the book and then the bricks.*) Is it a square?

A: Yes, that's right, a square.

C: (*Places two rectangles. Sits back on knees to observe the house.*) We need windows and a door. (*Places three square bricks as windows and a rectangle for the door. With A, takes a photograph of the house.*)

There are a number of features of this interaction that illustrate the kind of contingent support adults can give to encourage independent thinking and acting:

- Sally's assessment is focusing on what the child can do and she is keen to find out as much as possible though observation and interaction;
- she is not allowing the child to enter a dependency relationship with her;
- she alerts him to other supporting material in the context so that he should be able to work without her presence on a similar task in the future;
- she uses the language of shape and sets up opportunities for the child to do the same;
- she encourages, through her silences, the child's own evaluations of the work.

Sally has managed to ensure that the child remains in control of the activity and tailored support to the learning focus of the construction area. She has set up what Bruner refers to as the courteous conversations which support learning (Bruner 1996) and which acknowledge the importance of children's own search for meanings.

Bruner (1996: 57) explains how children are brought conversationally into the meaning making that is shared in their cultures:

> [children's] naive theories are brought into congruence with those of parents and teachers not through imitation, not through didactic instruction, but by discourse, collaboration and negotiation. Knowledge is what is shared within discourse, within a ... community ... this model of education is ... more concerned with interpretation and understanding than with the achievement of factual knowledge or skilled performance.

Bruner's view of how adults help young children as learners was certainly supported by our research partners who were anxious that too much of the *what* of learning would mean that they would have to work in inappropriately 'teacherly' ways with pre-school children. They wanted to focus on responsively helping children to make sense and act effectively in and on their worlds.

Learning occurs through the manipulation of the tools of a culture

This feature of a sociocultural approach to understanding learners and learning provides a useful framework for looking at resource-based pre-school provision. Cultural tools (Cole 1996; Wertsch 1991) include the meanings carried in the language we use – for example, referring to children as 'little' allows them to get away with breaking rules and is a reason for their being sent to bed before their older brothers and sisters.

Tools can be intellectual and include the way we think about activities – for example, the children in Alison's centre were encouraged to plan and evaluate. Also, cultural tools are the objects or artefacts with which we surround ourselves and with which we interact in culturally specific ways. For example, although pieces of wooden puzzles make good missiles, we offer them to children as puzzles and expect them to use them as such. Similarly, children are guided into participation in pre-school settings by learning the accepted way of using familiar materials, such as sand or water, while they are there. A focus on how language and artefacts are used can help practitioners identify how they can promote learning.

Every project in our research partnership in some way involved changing the use of existing resources in the various pre-school settings in order to make the most of the educational potential in them. In Molly's nursery the construction corner took mark-making as a focus and children recorded their achievements. Staff in Melissa's High Scope nursery school used 'play people' with the construction materials to support children's use of the language of position – for example 'inside', 'next to' etc. The mothers in Jenny's babies and books project found ways of using books with their children that they had not previously been aware of. In each of these examples the adults used familiar material in ways which exploited their educational focus. Also in each of these examples either Molly, Melissa or Jenny modeled for the other adults how the materials might be used.

In order for children to understand how material resources are used and learn the ways of thinking associated with them, they need to experience those resources in conversation with those who do have some understanding. So when first given a wooden puzzle children need to work on it with someone who will use it as a puzzle and not a missile store. While jointly assembling the puzzle, through trial and error or the sorting of pieces, children learn how members of their knowledge communities tackle such tasks. They learn not only the meanings of words 'here is another blue piece', but also how to approach the task by sorting, planning, testing and completing. They do this, as Bruner (1996: 57) suggests, through 'discourse, collaboration and negotiation', a set of ideas which is echoed in the Effective Provision of Pre-school Education (EPPE)'s 'sustained shared thinking' (Sylva, Melhuish *et al.* 2003).

The role of adults in guiding children into being competent users of the cultural tools of their society is therefore crucial (Edwards 2004b). In our partnership we concluded, the role is to open gateways to new understandings for children as they participate in the world around them. Opening gateways demands that adults journey alongside children and are themselves aware of the gateways and the opportunities that lie beyond them. They, therefore, cannot entirely escape the *what* of learning.

How children develop as thinkers

What goes on in children's minds is a fascinating field of study but we are probably still only at the 'best bet' stage of creating a complete framework for understanding children's thinking. We found that the insights into children as thinkers and learners offered by constructivism (a view that we construct our understandings of the world over time) and by sociocultural psychology (which focuses on how the cultural is incorporated into thinking and action), resonated with the experiences which were being recorded in the pre-school settings. We therefore worked selectively within these frameworks as we made sense of the children's experiences.

In this section we shall look at some of the features of the sense-making process. We shall focus on children as individual and as social thinkers.

Children as individual thinkers

The frameworks offered by Piaget for understanding how children process the information they glean from their experiences are 'best bets' and underpin most constructivist perspectives on children as learners (Wood 1988). The key words are *schema, assimilation, accommodation, equilibration* and *development.* These key concepts help us understand the processes of constructing understandings.

Schema, according to Piaget, are the mental structures into which we organize the knowledge we hold about the world. For example, 3-year-old Naomi playing in the water area might think that big things sink and small things float. She will have a sinking/floating schema, which although not in tune with expert knowledge, does work. The schema will change once she experiences enough counter evidence and needs another way of organizing that knowledge to make sense of the world.

Assimilation occurs when we take in information which does not demand that we alter our existing schema. For example, if another large object sinks Naomi won't need to adjust her schema. Assimilation can also occur when we experience something that is so beyond our capacity to understand it that we cannot engage with its meaning and therefore there is no impact on our schema. In the case of adults, this might be a discussion of time and space in the context of black holes.

Young children frequently find themselves in situations where they simply don't have the knowledge that allows them to make sense of an object or experience. We see this when children make 'music' with a keyboard, or mark-make when recording orders in the 'cafe'. We also see it when they turn an object to their own purposes and hand out leaves as 'cakes'. Much of children's play is assimilation and it is through this kind of imaginative play that children become familiar with the rituals and objects that are part of their worlds. Play of this kind is also important for adults. For example, many of us approach a new gadget by initially playing with it to see what it can do. But children need a great deal of assimilation-oriented play, as the familiarization with objects and how they might be acted upon is an essential part of sense-making.

Accommodation is what happens when we adjust our existing schema to take in new information. This is often simply a case of refining existing schema. For example, a child might eventually show by his language and behaviour that there is a schema that both he and adults call 'hat' and that his shorts do not now belong to it. Sometimes the adjustment is quite radical, demanding new schema, such as when Naomi recognizes that some large objects float and some small objects sink. A strictly Piagetian interpretation might argue that Naomi would manage the reorganization of her schema without adult help. A more educationally-oriented interpretation, and one we would advocate, would suggest that the adults' role is to provide the language support that helps children to recognize and label their new understandings. We saw an example of such support earlier in this chapter, in Sally's language when she helped the child to use the language of shape in the construction area.

Importantly, accommodation only occurs when the difference between existing schema and the new information is not too great. (Hence the importance of the opportunity for familiarization through imaginative play.) Problem-solving play is particularly valuable for encouraging accommodation of new information, as during this kind of play children are able to work using their existing schema on materials that have been selected to give them the opportunity to refine those schema. One should not, therefore, see assimilation and accommodation as distinct phases in a learning cycle that can be planned for. Rather they occur together when a child uses existing understandings and has to adjust them to be able to cope with new information. The sense-making process can, in this way, be seen as a search for a balance between what is understood and what is experienced.

Equilibration is the term used by Piaget to explain the constant adjustments made to schema by learners as they encounter events that disturb their current understandings and lead them to new explanations and a reorganization of the relevant schema. Sarah Meadows (1993: 203) usefully describes equilibration as 'the momentary non-functioning of a cognitive scheme [schema] which both signals the presence of a "perturbation" and is the sole motivator of efforts to seek a new equilibrium'. This definition nicely captures how a search for meaning motivates learners, and how contradictions between existing thinking and new interpretations take forward conceptual development. Both ideas are central to constructivist and to sociocultural approaches to learning.

Development is emphasized by Piaget to explain why very young children deal with events in qualitatively different ways from older learners. For example, they are much more likely to resort to intuition because they cannot hold two pieces of information in their minds and connect them. The thinking of very young children can, therefore, be seen to resemble a slide presentation in which each event is discrete. Only as they mature as thinkers do children develop the capacity to look backwards and forwards, to see life as more like a film and to make connections between distinct experiences. Stories and shared experiences that help recall and anticipation are therefore important to encourage more mature thinking.

Piaget's basic research question was 'How does knowledge develop in the minds of children?' Without a doubt he answered that question. His focus was therefore largely the description of development. He was not an educationalist and did not ask the question 'How are children helped to learn to participate knowledgeably in their cultures?' If that question interests us we need to turn to sociocultural psychology.

Children as social thinkers

We have already answered part of the question in our discussion of learning in context. In this section we focus on the processes children engage in as they get to grips with the world and the interpretations that others make of it. Key words here are *intermental, appropriation* and *collaboration.* The sources of these ideas are found in the work of Vygotsky and have been developed since by others who share Vygotsky's interest in how we can assist children as learners.

Intermental is used by Vygotskians to mean 'between minds', and reminds us of the social basis of human knowledge and its public display in our talk and actions. Vygotsky suggested that we first come into contact with knowledge through experiencing how others make sense of it but we then make it our own by connecting it to our existing understandings of the world by using it. Learners' understandings and actions can be guided both by others, who are able to highlight what is useful to select from the array of stimuli available to them, and by learners' own observations of how others in their knowledge communities behave.

A disposition to engage with the knowledge available is therefore clearly an advantage. But Vygotskians also emphasize the importance of language to learning, arguing that it assists the internalization of understandings. You might ask whether such a process is rather like the chicken and the egg. How can learners use language without understanding what it means? The answer to that question lies in appropriation.

Appropriation is what learners do when they use the language of their knowledge communities without necessarily understanding it in the way that more expert members do. This is often evident in imaginative role-play where children assume the language and mannerisms of the role and can be heard to *ventriloquize* the language of others. Appropriation of language occurs alongside imitation of behaviour and both appropriation and imitation help young children cope effectively with their worlds.

Observations in Alison's construction area produced several examples of younger children appropriating the language and imitating the behaviour of the older ones. For example, Harriet, aged barely three, picked up a pencil and paper and joined Connor and Ahmed in their mark-making record of their measurements of their boat. Jonty, also three, after observing the older boys, selected the larger blocks from the containers and made a 'pirate ship' with them.

Appropriation, together with imitation, is a very useful step in the journey towards individual understanding. Appropriation of the language used by others gives children access to the cultural tools that we outlined earlier and gives them experience of approaching tasks in the ways that their knowledge communities do.

Encouraging appropriation calls for attention to well-resourced role-play. It also requires a language-rich environment in which adults now and then think aloud in order to reveal how they are interpreting and responding to what is going on, so offering children the language formats that they can in turn ventriloquize when doing something similar. The importance of offering language in this way in home settings was made clear in the study by Wells (1987) discussed earlier in this chapter. It showed a strong positive relationship between the rate of language development at 30 months and the proportion of speech directed by mothers to the child in shared activities.

Shared experiences do seem to be a key to children's early development as thinkers. In pre-school settings these experiences are often created through neighbourhood walks and visits. From these activities, opportunities for recall and reconstruction are found in shared conversations around photographs taken while walking or visiting. These conversations, which move the child's thinking back to the past and forward to anticipate future events, assist young children's development as thinkers.

Collaboration between caregiver and infant is, as we have already outlined, the source of children's initial learning. We also know from studies of older children that constructive (as opposed to, for example, argumentative) collaboration, which allows children to build understandings together, also helps children develop as thinkers (Phillips 1985; Mercer 1995, 1996, 2000). However, gauging whether young children are able to collaborate fruitfully is difficult. In order to collaborate children need to understand that other people might see and interpret the same thing in different ways from them, and in trying to make sense of that difference, children develop their own thinking. This is quite an advanced thinking skill, requiring children to have senses of themselves as separate from others, who will in their turn be separate selves with their own interpretations, feelings and motives.

It is easy to both under- and overestimate children's abilities in this area. Judy Dunn's interesting work on children in their families from the age of 2 (Dunn 1988) has shown that from the third year of life children can be aware of the individual emotions and desires of close family members and respond appropriately. Dunn's more recent work (Dunn 2005) also highlights the importance of co-operative relationships in developing the ability to recognize the perspectives of others. This ability develops during the pre-school period. Our understanding of its importance has been increased by work on autistic children's *theory of mind* – that is, children's capacity to recognize that others will not just have separate feelings but also separate cognitions and so see things differently from them.

One way of assessing whether children have a theory of mind is to tell them stories in which one character believes something the children know is false, such as where an object is hidden. If children predict the character's action by recognizing that the character will follow the mistaken belief they can be said to have a reasonably well-developed theory of the minds of others (see, for example, Frith 1989). Children's responses to this form of assessment, in contrast to the way they operate in the more naturalistic settings observed by Dunn, suggest that they don't usually develop a robust theory of mind before the age of 4. However, a theory of mind is an essential attribute if children are to make the most of working together, rather than with an adult who is focusing on their interpretations.

In the following example we see how a pair of 4-year-olds in a reception class who are building a house using Duplo are beginning to explore each others' understandings and work collaboratively on the activity (the extract is taken from Ogden 1997).

Emma: Has your house got rooms with doors? Has it got three doors in the living room?

Sally: It's got one door in the living room and it's got ...

Emma: The door you go in?

Sally: And it's one door in the back kitchen, no, it's got two doors in the back kitchen, it's actually got three doors in the back kitchen.

Emma: So that means it's got three doors, that's the kitchen.

Work on theory of mind reminds us of the need for close and continuous observations of children when they are working together so that we can assess the development of children's theories of others' minds and can plan accordingly. Putting children together is not enough. We need to work with them to develop an ability to perspective take.

Learning and resilience

Learning is a process of increasingly informed participation in specific cultures and adults can do a great deal to promote children's learning through creating challenging environments and through sensitive attention to how children are interpreting and acting on their worlds. At the core of successful learning lie sound, responsive relationships between young children and adults. The study on which this book is based looked at learning literacy and number, that is the curriculum focus was strong. However all the statements we have made about relationships and the development of disposition hold good for children's broader emotional well-being, particularly their resilience or a capacity to persist and to deal with adversity. One cannot separate the emotional from the cognitive when supporting the early formation of children's minds. Early years practitioners, as we saw in the example of Ivy's project, are well placed to work collaboratively with practitioners from other services that are also concerned with building resilience.

In the next four chapters we use the frameworks discussed here to explore how young children develop their orientation to, and their participation in, literacy and mathematics.

Suggested reading

There is a vast amount of literature on children's learning from birth to 5 and a great deal of it focuses on how children learn in their social contexts.

A good introduction to this field is Schaffer, H.R. (1996) *Social Development* (Oxford: Blackwell). This text is aimed at undergraduate students and combines succinct accounts of major studies with a gentle explanatory style.

Cultural Worlds of Early Childhood is an excellent (1998) collection of work on children's learning in social contexts and is edited by M. Woodhead, D. Faulkner and K. Littleton.

Margaret Carr and Guy Claxton review work on learning dispositions in Carr, M. and Claxton, G. (2002) 'Tracking the development of learning dispositions', *Assessment in Education,* 9 (1): 9–37. This paper is also to be found in H. Daniels and A. Edwards (eds) (2004) *The RoutledgeFalmer Reader in Psychology of Education* which also includes chapters on sociocultural approaches to learning.

5   Language and literacy learning

Language and literacy in pre-school settings

One of the long-term aims of the project was to design curriculum guidelines in literacy and mathematical thinking for very young children. The processes by which we planned to achieve this aim were to identify: what activities the practitioners in their pre-school settings defined as literacy and mathematics; the nature of their understanding of how young children learn to be literate and numerate; and the relationship between early years workers' and parents' perceptions of how young children acquire competence in language, literacy and mathematical understanding. As we explained in Chapter 3, we used an action research model in our inquiry with the 20 practitioners in the project. Inevitably as we focused on what children were learning, we were drawn into discussions about how they were learning, and about how the adults were supporting their learning. The following four chapters will draw on the researchers' and practitioners' field notes and exemplary materials. Chapters 5 and 6 will focus on language and literacy and Chapters 7 and 8 on mathematical thinking.

The practitioners in the project brought with them distinctive preoccupations and discourses about language and literacy from their respective exo-system levels (see Chapter 1) of working traditions as childminders, carers and educators. Uniting care and education traditions at the micro-levels of their workplaces were essentially 'female' priorities and discourse about supporting families, forging caring relationships with children and their parents or carers and promoting the social/emotional development of the children. This discourse was set against references they made to the prevailing 'male' discourse of policy changes at the macro-level couched in terms of accountability for the spending of public money and promoting learning outcomes of a much more instrumental kind – for example, those in the discourse of the *Desirable Outcomes* document (DfEE/SCAA 1996). In 1996 this was the curriculum framework to which our practitioners were working.

The framework was superseded by a statutory Foundation Stage

curriculum for 3- to 5-year-old in 2000 (DfEE/QCA 2000). Both frameworks were designed to lead 4-year-olds into a subject-based National
Curriculum framework at school entry. In 1996, for practitioners in the
project with backgrounds in education (either within nursery nurse or
teacher training), the goals set out in the *Desirable Outcomes* framework
were relatively easy to absorb. However, it was clear from our dialogue
with practitioners from care sector backgrounds that for them the
document was intimidating.

Frances, the manager of an independent day nursery, described her
staff's reactions when she introduced the document at a staff meeting.
One responded to the mathematics outcomes with an anguished 'I
didn't even get me CSE in maths. I can't teach maths'; another to the
descriptors for knowledge and understanding of the world with a
worried 'I were crap at geography'. Other responses were more muted!
We found that some experienced practitioners from daycare settings
were apologetic about their perceived lack of knowledge about educational practice and their unfamiliarity with words such as 'curriculum'
and 'topics'. Others took a more assertive line and argued that they did
not want to be 'teachers'. For example, Sally, a deputy manager of a local
authority family centre, argued cogently:

> Some of our 4-year-olds are here with us for a long day. They've
> got all their school years ahead of them. We're not teachers.
> None of us has been trained how to teach a child to write their
> name, or read, or count. We did the basic things on NNEB
> courses; but we are not teachers and we don't feel qualified to
> teach those kind of things to the children. You hear horror
> stories about nurseries teaching the children the alphabet and
> then teachers have to re-teach them sounds – you know, they've
> been taught 'ay, bee, cee' and they want 'a, b, k' – and we're not
> teachers. But we can give them all the opportunities they need to
> prepare them for school.

In fact the children in this setting were offered well-planned and
stimulating activities covering a broad range of learning opportunities.
There was evidence of the experienced staff responding quickly to and
extending children's spontaneous episodes of learning. Again, Sally, the
deputy manager clearly articulated the strengths of the provision for
children's learning in the centre:

> We don't do much formal in the centre . . . but we cover the six
> [Desirable Outcomes for Learning] areas in play. We do science
> experiments. But we don't have the 4-year-olds coming out to do

tracing or worksheets or whatever. It's all done through fun, practical, play activities – tie-dying, baking, whatever.

At first the staff panicked when confronted with the requirements of an education-based curriculum. Their confidence in what they were achieving was undermined. Fortunately, an experienced early years adviser in the local authority reassured them that what they were offering the children was fine.

This episode gives us an insight into the fact that curriculum models are socially constructed. Adults design them with particular beliefs about what constitute appropriate activities for children at a particular moment in history. The beliefs of these adults emanate from the dominant values of the culture and society at the macro-level of Bronfenbrenner's model (see Figure 1.1, page 4) within which they live and work. But most significant in shaping their beliefs about what children should do and learn before school are the culture and ideologies of their training, professional backgrounds and daily work experiences at the micro-level of their early childhood workplace settings.

It was the distinctive belief systems of 'education' that were exemplified in the 1996 *Desirable Outcomes for Learning* definition of what young children should learn:

> The desirable outcomes are goals for learning for children by the time they enter compulsory education. They emphasize early literacy, numeracy and the development of personal and social skills and contribute to children's knowledge, understanding and skills in other areas. Presented as six areas of learning, they provide a foundation for later achievement.
>
> (DfEE/SCAA 1996: 1)

It is not surprising that those project members whose backgrounds were outside education felt threatened by the tone of *Desirable Outcomes for Learning*. The words were hard-edged – goals, compulsory education, literacy, numeracy, knowledge, understanding, skills, achievement. The definition was couched in terms of a 'high status' framework of preparation for academic achievements. Its focus was on the mind.

Contrast this set of goals for young children with one from the National Children's Bureau, where ideologies about childhood were framed in broader terms during this same period. The National Children's Bureau promoted the view that practitioners should draw families and communities into concerns about young children's development in a much more holistic way, and not just focus on their educational needs. A description of an appropriate curriculum for young children from one of their community of practitioners was 'investigation and exploration, walks and puddles and cuddles, books and blankets and anything that is part of a child's day, play and routines' (Rouse 1990). It is significant that there is a strong emotional component to this definition. The words used – cuddles, blankets, play – are about the physical and emotional needs of children, not just their intellectual needs. In this framework the body and the heart matter; the mind is just one part of the 'whole' child.

In the *Desirable Outcomes for Learning* (DfEE/SCAA 1996) document 'play' was scarcely mentioned. The language used was an indication of the construction of childhood that dominates our policy in early years services in the UK. 'Happiness' and 'play' tend to be derided by a male dominated society which emphasizes the logical, scientific aspects of learning and the power of rational thought (see Anning 2005b for further discussion of play and the legislated curriculum). Play is often dismissed as trivial or time wasting. Yet we argued in Chapter 4 that for early years practitioners play is perceived as the natural vehicle by which young children learn. In 1990 Fromberg, in his review of significant research evidence of the contribution of play to children's development pointed out, 'at the same time that the research literature on the value of play appears to expand geometrically the presence of play in early childhood classrooms has been dwindling' (p. 237). As the National Literacy Strategy imposed a set hour of literacy and numeracy teaching in primary schools for all 4- to 7-year-olds, opportunities for active, play based learning decreased (Anning and Ring 2004).

It is significant that education was assigned the lead role in the government's policy on integration of services for children. Throughout the 1990s, policies on early childhood education prioritized children's academic achievements (in particular their language and mathematical development), rather than their emotional and social development, or their physical well-being. Practitioners with educational backgrounds felt secure with these imperatives. So during the project, we never heard those with backgrounds in educational services apologize about their lack of knowledge and understanding of children's physical and emotional needs. We think these should be priorities. Even at a pragmatic level of measuring 'success', if children are not happy and comfortable, they are unlikely to feel good about learning and to make good progress in academic achievements. Equally, from a moral and ethical point of view, young children's emotional and physical well-being should be of paramount importance. It may be that those with educational backgrounds should learn from their colleagues in the care sector about catering for aspects of children's emotional and physical development. As the policies of integrating education, care and family support services were promoted strongly by the government in the early part of the new century, it was inevitable, and welcome, that the more broadly based Foundation Stage curriculum was introduced, with guidelines promoting the role of learning through play.

However, it was the discourse of 'school' subjects, not of children's general well-being, which dominated curriculum reform for young children for the two decades following the Education Reform Act of 1987. Of all the 'subjects' of the school curriculum, English is the one with which early childhood workers in all kinds of pre-school settings are most comfortable. However, depending on their backgrounds and belief systems, they will approach the 'subject' in rather different ways. For example, local authority funded daycare settings had a tradition of prioritizing language development in the activities they planned for their children. This emphasis was the result of the 'compensatory' framework of the care sector because, as we discussed in Chapter 1, historically their population was skewed to 'disadvantaged' families and children 'at risk'. However, childcare workers' approach to language development was very different from that in, for example, nursery classes in the maintained sector, where a particular 'school' view of language and literacy prevails with an emphasis on learning to read and write. In the childcare sector traditionally the focus was on the development of spoken language. As private childcare provision incorporating pre-school education has expanded in response the New Labour's promotion of public/private funding of childcare, the emphasis has swung more towards school activities in these settings in response to parental expectations of getting 'value for money' in purchasing pre-school services.

The foundations of the school concept of literacy are the nineteenth-century elementary school traditions of 'reading and writing'. Children were required to learn to write in 'a fair hand', often by laboriously copying poems from the established canons of English literature or morally uplifting tracts. They had to learn the discipline of parsing sentences in order to access the syntax of the English language. They had exercises in the comprehension and paraphrasing of high-status texts. Finally they learned to read from 'primers' of the Janet and John, Dick and Dora or Peter and Jane variety! All these activities were geared to the needs of training a docile working population ready to operate in working contexts where a particular, narrow version of literacy prevailed. Much of the nostalgic call for a 'back to basics' curriculum during the 18 years of Tory government in England and Wales up until 1996 was a hankering for a return to this simplistic notion of training a docile workforce. It could be argued that New Labour policy has simply added the word 'adaptable' to the requirement!

However, even if we were to accept the questionable view that the *raison d'être* of a curriculum is to prepare children for work, such a backward looking model takes no account of the rapidly changing nature of literacy in the twenty-first century. The computer, word processor, television, mobile phone and Internet have entirely altered the notion of what it means to be literate. Literacy is not simply a paper-based activity of reading and writing. We have to broaden our understanding to include the concept of multi-literacies (Cope and Kalantzis 2000). As Marsh (2004) argued in her study of young children's home-based literacy experiences, *'Embedded within children's literacy practices in the home were a range of popular cultural texts such as computers (mainly console) games, comics, books based on television characters and environmental print linked to media texts (stickers, video labels, computer game boxes and so on) (p. 53).'*

Television and videos also played a central role in the young children's experiences of narratives. Yet our education system is still geared to promoting literacy with a strong emphasis on 'conventional' reading and writing and this model is increasingly 'colonizing' pre-school settings (Miller 2001). The sign systems of school literacy – alphabet charts, words blu-tacked on to doors, chairs and tables, workbooks and worksheets – which set the boundaries of literacy in the formal settings of many early years classrooms have infiltrated the informal settings of family centres, privately funded daycare settings, childminders and even some young children's bedrooms or playrooms at home. Parents feel pressurized into joining this version of 'the literacy club' by a burgeoning industry in 'out-of-school'/homework educational materials. In supermarkets parents are urged to invest in an array of workbooks, videos and educational games, all designed to improve children's basic skills in reading and writing.

Since 1998 all children in primary schools of compulsory school age have been taught a formal 'literacy hour' every day. In September 1998, at the time of this project, even as children entered compulsory schooling (mostly at the age of 4) they were tested by baseline assessment systems on recognition of initial sounds in words, letters by both shape and sounds, and ability to write their names and words independently. Subsequently the baseline assessment of children has been moved to the end of the Foundation Stage as children transfer to Key Stage 1 at the age of 5. The assessments are much more broadly based and depend on practitioners in all settings offering pre-school education completing an elaborate Foundation Stage Profile (QCA/DfEE 2004). Nevertheless practitioners still feel particularly accountable for the results of children's literacy and numeracy scores on the profile. Young children and their parents learn to position themselves within this dominant model of literacy. For example, reading is perceived to be about decoding text in books. So Scollon and Scollon (1981) reported a young child explaining 'when my baby brother's hands are big enough to hold a book, he'll be able to read'.

We have to question both the appropriateness and effectiveness of this kind of curriculum model for language and literacy learning for young children. There are two aspects of the model that are questionable: the relationship of the model to what we know about children's *cognitive development* reviewed in the previous chapter and its relationship to what we know about the most *appropriate pedagogy* for young children.

Turning to *cognitive development* first, we know that children learn to use representational systems modelled by more expert learners – either adults or older children – in the social contexts in which they learn to be literate and numerate. Children experiment with different ways of representing their growing understanding of the world around them. In his seminal work on children's meaning making, Bruner (1963) identified three categories of representation. These were: *enactive* representations (when children participate through their actions), *iconic* representations (when they participate through looking at or making pictures or images of things) and *symbolic* representations (when they participate through using the more powerful symbols of, for example, print or mathematical symbols to represent things). Symbolic representations offer the child opportunities to move from consideration of the concrete here and now of immediate experiences to the abstraction of events that were in the past or may be in the future. The role of adults or more experienced siblings is to mediate for the child these different modes of representation until they are able to use them with confidence independently. They do so by modelling the use of different modes of representation (talking, gesticulating, drawing, scribbling notes) and giving feedback to children as they attempt to represent their own experiences and understandings. Bruner called this mediation 'scaffolding' (see page 00 in Chapter 4).

Piagetian stage theory seemed to indicate that young children have limited capacities to think at 'abstract' levels. However, Donaldson's (1978) seminal work, *Children's Minds*, argued that children could think at a high level of complexity and in abstract terms if the problems they tackled were embedded in contexts which made sense to them on an everyday, concrete level. Children were disadvantaged when confronted with problems that were 'disembedded' from their real world connections. One could argue that the kinds of 'school' literacy tasks presented to young children in print or mathematical notation form in early stages of their literacy learning were just such 'disembedded' problems. There is an argument that, by placing so much emphasis so early in a child's development on introducing them to the abstract symbolic systems of

.g meaning in print and numbers, we are wrong-footing them
ost vulnerable stage of learning to be learners. At this stage
opportunities to explore enactive (through storying and role-
p...,.   l iconic (through absorbing or making images of things)
representations.

The fact is that despite the current policy of promoting an early
introduction to 'school' versions of literacy, British children, particularly
boys, score less well on measures of achievements in language and
mathematics than children from systems in other European countries
where pre-school experiences place an emphasis on talk and structured,
active play which enable children to move more freely between enactive,
iconic and symbolic modes of representation. In these countries children
do not start their formal schooling with its emphasis on symbolic
representation until they are 6. For example in 2001 the Progress in
International Reading Literacy Study (PIRLS) comparative study of the
reading achievements of over 140,000 10-year-olds in 35 countries,
England ranked third below Sweden and the Netherlands. However, the
study indicated that English children were less likely to enjoy reading
than in the other countries in the study. Also England had the largest
variation between the most and least able children.

In 1998 researchers for a Channel 4 programme, *Britain's Early Years
Disaster*, tried to explore the consequences of expectation in this country
of children being exposed very early to symbolic modes of representation. They reported that:

> The evidence suggests that Britain's early years education, far
> from helping young children, actually damages many of them.
> Unlike successful pre-school systems abroad – which move
> slowly from the concrete to the representational and avoid the
> abstract – British early years provision rushes children into
> abstract letters, words and numbers. While elsewhere primacy is
> given to developing confidence and precision in spoken
> language, here teaching is dominated by reading, writing and
> recorded arithmetic.
>
> While brighter children and those from privileged back-
> grounds can cope with the demands this makes, less fortunate
> children suffer, lose confidence and probably never recover. It
> seems likely that this helps explain Britain's long tail of under-
> achievement. (Mills and Mills 1998: 17)

It is not only the curriculum content that may be inappropriate for
our young children, but also the danger that the pedagogy of early
childhood has become increasingly one of curriculum delivery. The

emphasis on 'direct instruction' and 'whole class teaching' in primary education, exemplified in the arguments for the National Literacy and Numeracy Strategies, impacted on reception and even some nursery classes in England and Wales. The EPPE project (Sylva Melhuish *et al.* 2003) was able to articulate what constitutes effective pedagogy in early childhood settings: 'sustained shared thinking' between adults and children, practitioners with a clear grasp of child development as well as good curriculum knowledge, the sharing of educational aims with parents, clear feedback for children in learning episodes and transparent behaviour policies and practice.

We have had research evidence that young children who are exposed to too formal a schooling regime too soon may suffer long-term disadvantages for some time. For example, results of the research in the USA (Schweinhart and Weikart 1993) cited in Chapter 2, page 00, reported by Sylva and Wiltshire (1993), indicated that three groups of children, one of which had experienced a formal pre-school curriculum and the other two play-based programmes (one a curriculum called High Scope and another less structured programme similarly based on active learning) showed increased IQs at school entry. However, in a follow-up study of the three groups at the age of 15, those that had attended the formal programme engaged more in antisocial behaviour and had lower commitment to school than those from the play-based programmes. Sylva (1997) again used research-based evidence to argue that 'a curriculum in pre-school settings that is too formal will lead to poorer performance, disincentives to learn and low self-esteem' (p. 4). This takes us back to the issues raised in Chapter 4 about the significance of promoting positive 'dispositions' in the crucial formative stages of children learning to be learners, including learning to be readers, writers and speakers.

Alternative approaches to literacy

So if 'school' models of language and literacy are inappropriate for under-5s, what models might be appropriate?

Chomsky (1976) argued that human beings are born with an innate ability to acquire language. He called this inborn mechanism a 'language acquisition device'. He argued that children build on their innate ability to learn language through interaction with the people around them and through engaging with everyday events and objects. Chomsky's work was crucial in developing our understanding of how individual children develop competence in language. However, in this project we took a *social-interactionist approach* to learning language and literacy. This approach is based on the view that the context scaffolds children's developing competence and that children are intentional communicators from very early on. The social and cultural setting in which a child acquires competence in talking, listening, reading and writing is as important as his or her individual developing competence in spoken language, or the ability to decode print, or to represent thinking in written form. Our approach acknowledges the active and purposeful role of babies in engaging adults in communication and the importance of the adult carer providing a language acquisition support system. Essentially, young children are motivated to use language formats in order to gain attention or to achieve some goal (Murray and Andrews 2000).

In Chapter 4 we saw how Ivy's work with babies, involving both parents and carers in a daycare setting, provided this kind of support to promote communication between babies and the adults who cared for them. Our approach acknowledged the importance of the pre-verbal communication system – gestures and sounds – established between babies and adults and siblings as a prerequisite for the development of language. These gestures and sounds, or early language formats, form a bridge to communication based on speech. They often take the form of games – for example, peek-a-boo or making growling or squeaking noises with soft toys.

However, *music and singing* can be an important pre-verbal mode of communication too. Babies play with the rise and fall, tone and pitch of sounds of language long before they use the spoken word to make meanings. Three members of the project (Frances, Millie and Jade) instinctively based much of their investigation on the role of songs and rhymes in very young children's learning. Frances used singing in many of her interactions with children. She described herself as 'a bit of a Pied Piper'. She was aware that singing and simple poems gave young children opportunities to communicate with adults and in small groups through sounds and speech, but without the pressure of meaning-making. The sounds in the songs and rhymes provided the children with 'scripts' to practise listening, making eye contact, turn-taking and responding.

Unless children are secure in the environment of a *rich oral culture* – what Egan (1988: 86) described as 'the lore and language, play and games, fantasy and story of young children' – their journey into literacy will be impoverished. Egan argued that 'sounds' of orality are powerful modes of binding generations together into shared understandings. He also urges adults to surround children with 'authentic' learning experiences rather than patronize them with what he describes as a 'baby safe' curriculum of activities designed exclusively for children. Interestingly, when Jade used songs as a mode for encouraging home/school collaboration with Somali and Yemeni families, she discovered that the concept of 'nursery rhymes' was not familiar to them. In their domestic lives everyone sang the same songs and heard the same music – lullabies for sleeping, religious chants for worship, rhythmical music for dancing. They did not have 'special' songs for children. Egan (1988: 86–7) wrote:

> We use endless formulae to impress an array of behaviour patterns on children, for road safety, cutlery and utensil use, care of toys and furniture etc. We recite proverbs, tell stories, teach rhymes, tell jokes etc. These all help to build the mental structures that systematize memory and poeticize the prosaic world, creating imaginative space and power to be enchanted by magic and ecstasy. If we begin to think of the objectives of our early childhood curriculum as tied up with magic and ecstasy, with imagination ... we might see our way to making literacy, numeracy, and rationality richer and more meaningful attainments.

The telling of *stories* is another important feature of a language acquisition support system. Familiarity with the structures of narrative forms – beginnings, middles and ends of stories – helps children to learn how to sequence ideas, remember the constituent parts of a series of past events and predict or anticipate what might happen to them in the future. In other words, stories provide for children a way of helping them think beyond the here and now of their immediate experiences to make that important leap to connections with a more distanced, abstract past or future (see Wells 1987; Paley 2004). Meek (1998) wrote '*in their own versions of stories children explore intellectually the nature of their own situation-childhood, and as they learn to become both the teller and the told, they are also learning to dialogue with their futures* (p. 18).'

Oral storying is often a rich and engaging feature of a family's everyday life – the banter about family rituals and quirks of character, the gossip on the telephone, the 'pub' talk, the recapping on the current soap opera crises. Children growing up in environments characterized by richness of oral language are drawn into a community of 'storying' and then replicate storying behaviours in their play. Paley, in her earlier work, (1986: 124) reported her eavesdropping on such a community of young fluent speakers:

> The children sounded like groups of actors, rehearsing spontaneous skits on a moving stage, blending into one another's plots, carrying on philosophical debates while borrowing freely from the fragments of dialogue that floated by. Themes from fairy

tales and television cartoons mixed easily with social commentary and private fantasies, so that what to me often sounded random and erratic formed a familiar and comfortable world for the children.

Storying based on books is another key experience for young children learning to be literate. If adults read stories to children, at bedtime at home or in story reading sessions in playgroups, they are inducting children into the fun of book behaviours as well as the conventions of print. Fiction has a particular set of linguistic conventions: for example, 'Once upon a time' and 'So they all lived happy ever after'. Gaining familiarity with these conventions helps children to 'tune into' the kind of reading and writing they will be expected to do when they start school.

Heath's seminal (1982, 1983) study of the language use of families in different communities in the USA identified that families defined as middle class were more likely to model the kind of 'learning and displays of knowledge expected in school' (Heath 1982: 51). In many of the families in her study defined as working class, encounters with books or what she described as 'major literacy events' for the children were more likely to be based on didactic-style reading of alphabet or number books or Bible stories. Inevitably those children who are familiar with the rituals of 'school' story reading are at an advantage when starting school. In the UK Weinberger (1996) studied the home reading habits of sixty 3-year-olds from a wide variety of social backgrounds. Almost all the children had books at home. Many had favourite books, often based on stories or characters from Disney videos or television characters. These texts were often 'ephemeral', bought at supermarkets on impulse during the weekly family shop, 'read' till they dropped to pieces to be superseded by another favourite. The reading diet of the children at home was often very different from the canon of 'good quality' books found in the reading corners of many early childhood settings. Yet these favourite books at home often held great personal meaning for the child. They were often disappointed that when they brought them into their early childhood setting, practitioners were not keen to read them at story times. Wilkinson's (2003) studied the reading preferences of four young children and the impact of parents' preferences in children's books on family reading behaviours. Parents' preferences for reading to their children were frequently negotiated with the children who had very specific personal reading interests.

So we can see that what counts as literacy is co-constructed in the minds and daily activities of parents or carers, teachers and children. Versions of literacy are dependent on the social contexts in which they are enacted. For example, the rituals of book-based reading will be very different when a parent is reading a child a bedtime story, or when a playgroup worker is reading a story to a group of children sitting on a mat before 'home time', or when a teacher is listening to a child reading from her or his reading scheme book.

The project team took the view that the model of beginning *reading* that most benefits young children is not the 'disembedded' learning of letter sounds and names and the completion of phonic-based work-sheets, but reading within the context of enjoying story and picture books, and delighting in the telling and retelling of familiar fairy stories and rhymes. Playing with sounds, rhythms and words whets children's appetite for learning about all aspects of language. At this stage (and still) arguments about the relative value of teaching phonics through synthetic or analytic approaches were still being waged (HMSO 2004, 2005). Analytic phonics is embedded in the National Literacy Strategy. Unlike synthetic phonics, the approach using analytic phonics does not necessarily break words down into the smallest sound units. Rather it divides words into opening (onset) and closing sounds (rime), as in str-eet. In synthetic phonics the same word would be broken down into five components, s-t-r-e-e-t. However, English is bedeviled by erratic relation-ships between letters and their sounds. It would seem sensible at the early stages of teaching phonics to focus on beginning and ending sounds of words. Later we can tackle the phonemes (smallest units of sound in a word represented by one or more letters, such as sock or shoe) and diagraphs (two letters representing one phoneme, as in ba*th* and *tr*ain) that children will encounter regularly.

We took the view that children learn much of their literacy before school from opportunities to engage with functional literacy in everyday situations – recognizing well-known sounds, signs and symbols as well as significant words and numbers from everyday life: advertising jingles, soap opera theme music, Coke bottle signs, supermarket logos, car registration numbers, street signs, letters and numbers on the TV screen. A theme tune becomes associated with family watching the television together, a letter K with a favourite cereal at breakfast time and the Little Chef logo with a meal-break in car journeys to grandma's. Children are exposed to all kinds of information systems – sounds, signs, lists, moving images on computer or television screens. They are exposed from babyhood to a world of multi-modality and multi-literacy. In compar-ison, the world of 'letteracy' in school must seem rather dull.

As for *writing*, again we took a much broader view of communication through graphic form than that associated with 'school' writing. Young children's attempts to externalize their understanding may take the form of mark-making, manipulating objects, making models, drawing or role-play behaviours. We were informed particularly by the work of Kress (1997) who argues that 'Children act multi-modally, both in the things they use, the objects they make; and in their engagement of their bodies; there is no separation of body and mind' (p. 97). We have subsequently found Pahl's (2002) work helpful. In her ethnographic study of three young boys at home she explored the way space was contested between the boys and their parents on the 'cusp of mess and tidiness'. The boys moved freely from playing with toys, found materials, role-play in front of the TV and mark-making. She saw the ability for the boys to move fluently from one activity to another as they created meanings as a real benefit of home based learning. Both Kress and Pahl argue that it is through multi-modal representations of their understanding that young children move confidently towards literacy.

Young children move freely between expressing themselves through spoken language, mark-making, making models, manipulating objects in role-play and physical movements. Athey's (1990) work on schemas developed the idea of 'patterns of repeatable behaviour into which experiences are assimilated and that are gradually co-ordinated' (p. 37). She categorized the types of schemas she observed 2- to 5-year-old children using in nursery and home settings – for example, 'dynamic circular', 'enclosure', 'developing and containing space', 'dynamic vertical'. She claimed that schemas exemplified in children's mark-making were replicated in their play behaviours. So, for example, if a child were preoccupied with a 'dynamic circular' schema, she or he could be observed repeatedly drawing circles, playing in sand and water using circular movements, rolling a ball, rotating and staring at wheels on bikes or prams or running in circles, and would be particularly interested in songs (such as 'Round and Round the Garden') or stories (such as 'The Enormous Turnip') in which circular shapes figured.

Children's first experiments with *mark-making* are for kinaesthetic pleasure – making patterns on their high-chair tray with jam-covered fingers or later moving crayons across the surface of paper (Anning 2002; Matthews 1994). As when adults shape babies' babbling into speech sounds by feeding back to them with delight sounds that approximate to words (mum, mum mum or da da da) so adults feed back interest in the marks children make when they begin to create more controlled patterns. So a circular scribble becomes a face and horizontal and vertical marks become a house. The child is encouraged to make the crucial shift to using marks to represent things by the reactions of adults or older children, by their modelling of drawing behaviours or their feedback as young children made their own first attempts to draw.

However, while they are being socialized into the use of conventional forms of representation, children continue to explore their own personal and essentially private agenda through making compositions which often involve accompanying talk and actions (Anning and Ring 2004). Some of their marks represent sounds (the pitter-patter of rain may be dashes), or movement (the path of a spaceship represented by a long sweeping line), or emotions (dark, frenzied scribbling to black out the figure of a newly-born rival sibling). These marks are the visual equivalent of dramatic play where objects (cushions, tablecloths, pieces of furniture, soft toys) become the physical manifestations of the child's imaginative world. There have been some detailed studies of the unique pathways young children have taken towards drawing capability, usually documented by parents but also by researchers (for example, Matthews 1994; Anning and Ring 2004).

There are parallel detailed longitudinal studies of children's journeys towards literacy (for example, Bissex 1980; Baghban 1984; Laminack 1991). Children learn about *writing* by watching adults and older children writing. Their mark-making approximations that lead to letter shapes therefore reflect the configurations of the writing that are dominant in the culture in which they are growing up. Gregory's (1996, 1998) research on young bilingual children cites some examples of young children's emergent writing in two versions of scripts at both home and school. Children's approximations of letters are gradually shaped into recognizable letters, which are then combined into words and then sentences. Their first written words are those that are related to their burgeoning sense of self and to key relationships or objects in their everyday lives – their own names, significant TV characters, favourite animals, key members of the family. In home contexts young children are involved in multiple forms of social communication, linking drawing with writing, text messages with sounds, screen images with songs. Wollman-Bonilla (2001) contrasts the 'alternative hybrid text models' of home-based literacy episodes to the narrow versions of 'writing instruction' that characterize early learning in school settings.

Children then learn sound/letter relationships in order for them to be able to invent novel letter sequences which convey meaning to other people. Two seminal research programmes by Clay (1975) and Ferreiro and Teberovsky (1982) reported how children develop understanding of the alphabetic nature of writing systems. They charted young children's attempts to create messages. Children use letter names to convey speech sounds – for example the famous note pushed in front of Bissex (1980) by her young son when she repeatedly ignored his attempts to get her attention: 'RUDF' (Are you deaf?). The children used mainly consonants at first. Vowels appeared later. They tended to group letters into units of three or four to make their first 'words'. As their knowledge of written language grew, they gained increasing confidence in making their messages clear. Adults play a crucial role in being the audience for such messages and in responding to them with written or spoken replies. It is important for adults to encourage children in their initial idiosyncratic attempts at 'emergent writing' and to guide them gently towards the conventions of print.

It is also important to encourage children to experiment freely with communicating through drawing, making models and making images on computer screens. By the time our young children are adults, literacy will look very different. Increasing reliance on information retrieval systems which use diagrams, sounds and both still and moving images to convey meaning will generate very different demands on the next generation of writers. As Kress (1997: 142) argues 'The world into which children will move will be a world of multi-modality and multi-literacy. It will demand such skills and dispositions as part of an adaptable, innovative workforce'.

The co-construction of a new literacy curriculum

The problem for practitioners in informal, non-school settings, as many in our project were, is that as yet the discourse about young children learning in informal settings in their professional literature was in its infancy. As Munn (1994a) pointed out, before children enter schooling the curriculum will often be based on activities that are about practical skills (such as learning to get shoes on and off), social skills (such as taking turns in card or board games) or about learning the routines of being in an institutional setting (such as eating together). Such 'knowledge' has not been codified and is often dismissed as 'trivial'. In order to give such knowledge status, educators work backwards from 'school' knowledge and retrospectively justify these activities in educational terms. Munn gave the following examples:

- buttoning up coats involves one-to-one correspondence and therefore maps on to counting;
- tying shoelaces involves spatial awareness and therefore maps on to mathematical development;
- distinguishing colours and shapes involves perceptual discrimination and therefore maps on to reading.

As she pointed out, 'By such extrapolation, cognitive aspects of the preschool curriculum are created from basic tasks and an educational discourse is constructed' (Munn 1994a: 7).

However, this construction of an 'educational discourse' leaves early years workers from non-school settings feeling disempowered. It may also mean that they do not engage meaningfully with formal curriculum documents. In Blenkin and Kelly's (1997) analysis of returns from a range of settings providing for children from birth to 8 within their *Principles into Practice in Early Childhood Education* project, many practitioners, including those from Key Stage 1 settings, did not respond to the question 'How would you describe a quality curriculum for young children?' Others simply appended local authority or national guidelines for curriculum coverage. The documents had become a reason not to think any more.

What was important for us was to try to promote an exchange of ideas between practitioners from family centres, family support workers, childminders and practitioners from nursery education settings. We wanted them to address a new version of the curriculum which would not dismiss routine activities as 'trivial' or recast them as 'preparation for school learning'. We wanted to build on the knowledge and expertise embedded in their workplace practices, rather than base a dialogue on imported, disembedded curriculum models. We wanted to co-construct a curriculum from their authentic work-based practices.

In order to confront the similarities and differences between the perceptions of the care- and education-based practitioners in the project, and to confront the prejudices each may have had about each other's work-based practices, it was important that each sector had direct access to evidence of what the other actually did in promoting literacy. Only when assumptions were confronted by evidence could defensive posturing and mutual suspicion begin to break down. It is to this evidence, and to the role of the adults – both at home and in pre-school settings – in promoting children's learning in language and literacy that we turn in Chapter 6.

Suggested reading

A comprehensive introduction to language and literacy education in the early years is Marian Whitehead's *Language and Literacy in the Early Years: An Approach for Education Students* (Paul Chapman Publishing Ltd: 1990).

Eve Gregory's edited collection *One Child, Many Worlds: Early Learning in Multicultural Communities*, published by David Fulton in 1997 includes 11 case studies of children aged 3 to 8 in a range of cultures (UK and international) entering the culture and language of schooling.

Jackie Marsh and Elaine Millard's book, *Literacy and Popular Culture: Using Children's Culture in the Classroom*, published by Paul Chapman in

2000, discusses new approaches to literacy learning including techno-literacies.

For the beginnings of reading and writing, Robin Campbell's short but accessible *Literacy in Nursery Education* published by Trentham Books in 1996, sets out models of good practice in nursery schools. Linda Miller's more comprehensive *Towards Reading*, published by Open University Press in 1996 brings together recent research on early literacy development and implications for practitioners. For the beginnings of writing both Gunther Kress's *Before Writing: Rethinking the Paths to Literacy*, published by Routledge in 1997 and Kate Pahl's *Transformations – Children's Meaning Making in the Nursery*, published by Trentham Books in 1999, are excellent.

Pathways to Language: From Foetus to Adolescent by Karmiloff and Karmiloff-Smith, published in 2001 by Harvard University Press, is a good general introduction to language development.

6 How adults support children's literacy learning

Some examples from the project

In each of the diverse settings where the project team worked on Step 2 (see Figure 3.1) of the action research cycle they began by collecting evidence of literacy activities in the workplace and considering how these compared to the children's language experiences in the informal learning contexts of home. Their first surprise was how much was currently going on in their normal working activities with very young children that corresponded to the broad definition of literacy set out in Chapter 5. So we found that there was much to build on in the *what* content of 'everyday' literacy activities in their daily interactions with babies, toddlers and 'pre-school' children: enjoying books together, mark-making in role-play areas, chatting about the daily routines around snacks, washing their hands, tidying up the toys and equipment, setting off for walks to the shops.

There was less confidence about how to structure and organize the *how* of the curriculum – how to plan for enrichment activities without losing the spontaneity and enthusiasm shown by the children for self-chosen tasks; how to monitor and record children's progress in a way that was both useful and manageable; how to improve the quality of staff/children interactions; how to share understandings of emergent literacy with parents/carers.

However, the important thing was that all the questions raised were based on the documentary evidence of observations of staff and children working together in authentic contexts and under the real constraints of the hectic nature of working in pre-school settings. These questions were the starting points for the second cycle of action research when 'hunches' about possible answers were tested against further evidence gathered during Step 3 of the project.

Two such starting points are illustrated in the descriptions of projects given below. They were situated in very different types of settings, and illustrate, in summary:

- how two practitioners worked through the action research cycle towards clarifying their approach to developing a literacy curriculum for very young children;
- the important principle of involving work colleagues in the processes of action research and working closely with them to manage change;
- the principle of involving parents in young children's development and learning.

Example 1

Frances was the manager of a thriving workplace nursery. She had initiated a shift from family grouping into areas for separate age groups: for example, areas for under-2s and over-2s. In 1998 we found such regrouping of children into same-age 'bands' common in early years/family centres, as staff prepared for Ofsted inspections focused on their 'delivery' of the 1996 *Desirable Outcomes for Learning* (DfEE/SCAA 1996). The regrouping of the children had created a great upheaval in the nursery, and Frances was aware that the staff were keen to monitor the effects of the reorganization on the children. For example, one of the anxieties about the 'banding' of children was that it might restrict their flexibility in reorganizing age groups during daily routines.

Frances set up a meeting between herself and two members of staff. They discussed their concerns about some children's lack of turn-taking and listening skills and the possibility of using an expanded repertoire of singing, action rhymes and percussion work to improve them. Notes in her research diary show a clear sense of purpose: 'Our aim was to value and expand our children's ability to listen, communicate and interact.'

The vehicle they chose to achieve this aim was music. Frances believed passionately that music was undervalued in young children's learning. She believed that singing and making music had great potential to provide 'scripts' for communicating in speech, encouraging children to listen carefully and extending their ability to pay attention for longer periods. In fact there is research evidence that learning nursery rhymes, clapping rhythms and playing action and marching games encourages children to listen for and recognize rhymes and rhythms in speech. These skills help them later to acquire the more formal knowledge of phonics and syllables in words in the beginning stages of learning to read (see Goswami and Bryant 1990; Trevarthen 2000).

One of the 'hunches' the two members of staff wanted to test was whether older children offering models of more expert listening, turn-taking and singing or making music in mixed-age activities was beneficial to the younger children. They began to observe the under- and over-2s, sometimes singing together as a mixed group, sometimes in much smaller same-age groups. Examples of their dated observations are given below. Frances collated them as the starting point for discussion at the next staff meeting.

> Mixed ages and target children held hands and sang 'Ring-O-Roses'. Sat in a circle to sing five more songs together. All happy except G (aged 1) who crawled away after one song. Distracting to have younger children when I'm working with my target group (Laura: 19.8.97).

> Children all gathered on the carpet. Sang 'Twinkle Twinkle', 'Heads and Shoulders', 'If You're Happy and You Know It'. All eager to join in. I did the actions wrong once or twice to see if they'd notice – the older children did! I watched who knew the actions and who didn't. Lots of fun. Then we went on to some number games: 'Five Little Astronauts', 'Five Currant Buns'. Enjoyed the first one, but then they started to get distracted. They could see the new toys being put out for the after dinner activities. I observed it was much easier to hold their attention when everyone was joining me with the actions rather than some watching others do things (Ruth: 12.8.98).

In her notes, Frances, as the manager of the nursery, indicated the complex relationship between improving the quality of children's learning experiences and planning for the professional development of individual members of a staff team. In her notebook she wrote:

> I wanted to ensure collaboration between the rooms and see that a chasm did not occur. I also felt sure the link for the rising 2s would be excellent. The two key staff I had selected had not had the opportunity to work closely together and since they were both strong characters, I hoped they would influence others.

The staff shared their notes at a second meeting. They began to see patterns in children's behaviours in both the mixed- and single-aged groupings. Frances wrote:

> We noticed differences in which children were able or willing to join in the activities and remember the words/sounds. We noted who had the confidence to sing alone in the small same-age

groups but not in the larger group. We were surprised at how quickly they all grasped the rituals of sitting in a circle or the actions of the finger rhymes in the mixed-age groupings. We began to note changes in behaviour of children at story times who were now beginning to listen better. Did Lauren do so well in settling to stories now because she'd been part of our target singing group? Or was she just ready to be attentive in a group story time now?

The singing activities led to a book of nursery songs and rhymes being printed for the parents so that they could enjoy at home the songs and rhymes the children were learning in the nursery. The book became a point of contact when these busy working parents came to collect their children. On a superficial level the talk around handing the songbooks backwards and forwards between parents and practitioners was about non-threatening, fun activities that they could all share in and enjoy; but the chatting gave opportunities to raise some significant issues about individual children's learning and development for staff and parents. For example, Frances noted an exchange between herself and the parent of a particularly confident singer – so confident that despite her small stature she had been observed frequently directing other children at music making or singing times. The child's father was able to play an instrument. The child was due to leave the nursery shortly because a second baby was due in the family. It was during these informal exchanges about the songbook that he promised to encourage her love of music in every way possible.

The focus on music led to the two members of staff setting up a rhythm station in a corridor for children and parents to explore sound together. Staff also set up a tape deck so that children could select and play their favourite music. The staff negotiated with some local businesses to sponsor the production of some large 'song and game mats' to lay out in corridor areas used for large motor play when it was too wet or cold to play outside. At all stages of the project observations were made of the children using these new resources to feed back into the next phase of planning. Photographs and video recordings were used to supplement field note observations. The cycle of planning, recording, evaluating and re-planning meant that the curriculum experiences offered to the children were constantly being improved or refined. A section of a display board for parents in the nursery entrance hall kept them informed of what the staff were finding out about the children and their music making. The parents and staff planned an evening of seventies music together. In her final evaluation of the project Frances noted:

Our aim to value and expand our children's ability to listen, communicate and interact has been achieved. But music now has a higher profile in the nursery with a variety of practical games/props to use. We also have a staff team who are I believe more aware of the huge benefits music can make to everyone's lives.

Example 2

Meg was the manager of a very different setting, an inner-city early years centre. She had a clear vision of the role of the centre:

'The children's development and education are not looked at in isolation. The child is part of a family unit and the community in which s/he lives. We consider our role as one of family supporters and educators of children.'

Through questionnaires and informal discussions with parents about their approaches to supporting their children's development, Meg understood that they did not want to be involved in working with their children in the centre. She discovered that they made little use of the local library. However, it was clear that they wanted the best start in life for their children.

The records and monitoring systems in the centre showed that a high percentage of the children had poor social skills and behaviour problems. They also had poor speech, listening and comprehension skills. They showed little evidence of having handled books or of positive attitudes towards them.

Meg decided to take up a local authority initiative to support early years centres in setting up book loan schemes for families. She saw it as a way of addressing several challenges: stimulating the children to enjoy books, involving parents in their children's early literacy learning, and providing a vehicle to enhance the communication between staff and parents/carers.

The book loan scheme proved to be a great success with the parents. It gave plenty of opportunities for the staff to capitalize on the good informal relationships they had built up with parents. As with the chat around the songbooks in Frances' setting, the chat around the weekly early morning session set aside for selecting and returning books provided non-stigmatized opportunities for dialogue between staff and parents about many aspects of children's development, but particularly about sharing books with them. In this context (as in Frances', where parents were in full-time work) setting up 'workshops' to support parents in 'how to teach children about reading' would have 'frightened parents off'. Instead they designed some simple, non-jargon prompt sheets for parents to take home when they were choosing books. Such informal, user-friendly support for the parents worked well. The prompt sheets included such suggestions as:

- find quiet moments for sharing books;
- even babies enjoy playing with books – they won't tear them if you show them how to hold them;
- don't nag if you're both not enjoying it – stop and try again another time.

Meg noted at the end of several months of monitoring the book loan scheme:

> Children are instigating conversations about books they've read at home with parents. They are eager to borrow new books and ask 'Is it book loan today?' Parents are saying things like 'I must have read this three hundred times! I know it off by heart.' There is a noticeable improvement in how children are handling books in the centre. The book loan sessions have offered opportunities for parents to talk about their own literacy and how they can extend the help they have been giving when their children learn to read and write. It has offered them opportunities to discuss concerns they have about their children's language and speech. Books have also helped them over difficult issues to deal with – bed wetting, potty training, sharing, daddy leaving home etc.

Once the book loan scheme was firmly established, the staff wanted to introduce something new to the scheme. When one of the researchers mentioned the power of nursery rhymes in young children's develop-ment towards literacy, the staff decided to introduce nursery rhyme cards into the loan scheme. The rhymes were word processed in large type on to colourful cards and suggestions for shared activities between the parent or carer and child were added to the back of each card. Suggestions included actions to accompany the rhymes, finding familiar words together, pointing along the lines as you sing the words, missing out some words and letting the child add them, making up some 'silly' alternative rhymes of your own. (The latter suggestion was given the thumbs down by the parents as too hard!)

Particularly full records were kept of a 3-year-old child, Mandy, a child referred by social services, and her parents' responses to the books and nursery rhyme cards loan scheme. Mandy's parents said that they had not enjoyed reading at school and were not confident readers now. For them reading aloud to Mandy did not bring back happy memories at first, but as they pointed out, 'at home no one can hear you'. Mandy was very demanding of her parents' attention and often had temper tantrums. Sharing books provided a point of contact between her and her parents. As Meg noted:

> When there are difficulties at home that are not child-centred, it is hard at times for Mandy to compete for attention. The books help her parents to focus attention on Mandy. Mandy has also realized that one way of gaining her parents attention as an alternative to temper tantrums is using books. Her parents have also used sharing books as a way of calming her down. They have found 'Bartholomew's Potty' a real help; the knowledge that potty training and temper tantrums are not unique to Mandy. 'Bartholomew's Potty' is about saying no, no, no. The big teddy in the story stays calm throughout (parent role model?) and lets Bartholomew get on with it. Eventually he uses the potty . . . The close contact that reading together requires, sitting on your knee, making eye contact, cuddling up together, has helped the relationship between Mandy and her parents. The book loan and the rhyme cards have allowed the child and parents to play together. When an adult is presented with a toy to play with a child, the role of the adult is not easily defined. A toy is a child's domain and the adult may not feel comfortable with it. Sharing a book is much more a natural shared activity.

Comments from Mandy's parents included:

> She will try to make up the story she sees in the pictures in her own words. I read the book first then Mandy tries to read it to me. She will try sounds and copy me. She has never done this before. She was having to see a speech therapist.
>   The nursery rhyme cards are good. She now sings all the time. We didn't know many nursery rhymes before but we do now.

At the end of the project Meg reviewed the impact of the book and rhyme cards loan scheme on the centre. Key findings were:

> The setting up of the book loan and the introduction of the rhyme cards did not produce instant results. Far more important was the consistency of the twice a week sessions and the availability of a member of staff to promote discussion with the

parents and value and respect their views. However, there was an increase in parents' interest in their children's ability to become literate and they were increasingly observant about what their children could do; for example, 'She can recognize the first letter of her name now.' It allowed children to make choices about books and stimulated their curiosity about them. Some children have started to bring their own books into the centre with them. The dialogue with parents gave the staff the opportunity to value early years education in its own right, not just as a stopgap while children are waiting to go to school.

There is plenty of research evidence that involving parents in young children's literacy learning through home visits and workshops is beneficial for children's confidence and competence as beginning readers and writers. See, for example, Weinberger's work in Sheffield (Weinberger *et al.* 1990); work done in Birmingham within the Shopping to Read Programme (Strongin Dodds 1994); the Basic Skills Agency's family literacy programmes evaluated by the National Foundation for Educational Research in 1994–5 (Brooks *et al.* 1996). However, the work of Meg and her staff is a fine example of how staff in an early childhood setting which has by tradition been more focused on care than education can acknowledge and build on what parents do at home. As Strongin Dodds (1994: 12) argued, parents can, by informal but highly skilled intervention, be empowered to be significant 'teachers' of their children if they are given appropriate support: 'It is not that they lack the initiative, but they are uncertain about the practicalities of teaching their children.'

As we pointed out at the beginning of this chapter it was the 'practicalities of teaching', the *how* adults support children's learning to be literate, that most taxed the early years workers in the project. We shall examine how they set about exploring their roles as educators using as an organizing framework the age phases members of the team chose to focus on (see Table 3.1, page 34): birth to 18 months, 18 months to 3 years and 3 years to 5 years.

Birth to 18 months

Communication through speaking and listening

Ivy managed an early years' centre set in a deprived inner-city area. She had a social worker background. In her project an important premise was that parents were offered support in a way that was respectful of, rather than a denial of, their personal and domestic realities. Many of the families in the community were beset by multiple difficulties with housing, money and relationships. Ivy was concerned about the effects of acute depression, suffered by some of her most vulnerable parents, on their communication with their babies. In her notes she wrote: '*I want to develop in parents the skills and knowledge that they are the ones best able to facilitate their own children's development. It is also important to acknowledge and understand the stress and pressures on individual families.*'

Ivy was also concerned that her staff were not generally given effective training in how to work with babies. Her experience was that qualifications and courses tend to emphasize training early years workers for the needs of 3-year-olds and upwards. Thus, though Ivy made her project focus communication skills between mothers and babies, the centre's development plan included upgrading staff expertise in their communication with babies.

Ivy targeted six mothers categorized as having learning difficulties themselves or whose babies were identified as 'at risk'. Although she was extremely competent and confident in how to work with families from her social work perspective, she felt less sure about her understanding of how to promote language development with babies. Wisely, she drew on the expertise of colleagues in the meso-system of the community of practice around the centre: the speech therapist attached to the centre, the health visitor, the course tutor from the speech therapy department of the local college and a local nursery teacher. Between them they designed and contributed to six workshops for the mothers: 'Getting to know each other', 'Singing nursery rhymes', 'Noise-makers and listening', 'Talking with baby', 'Listening and looking out of doors' and 'Reviewing what we have done'.

The workshops were planned in detail, but the delivery was deceptively relaxed and informal. Ivy and her colleagues from other agencies understood the importance of modelling 'motherese' and were not afraid to muck-in to demonstrate how to play with babies. The workshops were scheduled one morning a week for six weeks for two hours. This allowed time for a cup of coffee and a snack for the babies and some relaxed chat as well as the workshop 'proper'. The mothers were cautious at first and attendance at the workshops was erratic. Nevertheless, Ivy kept the workshops running as planned. She video-taped some of the later sessions when everyone had learned to have fun without feeling inhibited. When Ivy shared the video extracts with the rest of the project team later, it was wonderful to see the gradual unfreezing of the mothers' tense faces and stiff bodies as they learned to enjoy the communication games with their babies.

Ivy encouraged the mothers to use the instant camera provided in the centre to record what they did at the workshops and stick the photographs into a scrapbook made out of a simple lined exercise book. These exercise books became significant objects for the mothers. We were allowed to borrow them for the project only on the promise that they would be returned to them in pristine condition. For once in their lives the ability of these women to 'mother' was being validated instead of questioned. The evidence of their growing confidence in communicating with their babies was captured in the video extracts and the notes they entered alongside the photos in their exercise books. This evidence made a strong impact on the whole project team. It was profound in its ordinariness.

Ivy began to pull together the insights she had gained into curriculum guidelines for speaking and listening with babies. Her notes formed the basis of a chart, to which many others in the project eventually contributed, showing how principles in supporting young children's learning in literacy can be translated into practice.

Underpinning these principles was the recurrent theme of paying due attention to the affective responses of adults and children in institutional settings and at home. Practitioners have always understood the power of emotions in learning, but researchers have been slow to investigate this most complex of fields. As Kress (1997: 110) pointed out, 'At the moment we know little about all of this: and we know very little because the issue is not quite respectable on the public agenda.' Ivy knew that a lack of sound, affective communication between babies and adults was a danger for her own staff as well as for the children's mothers. Her gut feeling is borne out by research evidence.

Peter Elfer and Dorothy Selleck (Elfer *et al.* 2003) emphasize the importance, during what we called in Chapter 4 the 'intersubjective phase' of children's development, of key adults forming authentic emotional relationships with the children in their care. These authentic emotional relationships are reflected in the quality of speech interactions between adults and children and in their participation in joint involvement episodes (Schaffer 1992). Hopefully their 'conversations' with babies will involve them in the dynamic kind of language formats (Bruner 1983) also discussed in Chapter 4. Sadly, the data from Elfer *et al.* (2003), based on analysis of 150 hours of observations of babies in 15 nurseries indicated that where organizational systems allocate care workers to attend to the needs of too many babies, workers are driven to depersonalize their relationships with them. They concentrate on the 'presenting' needs of the babies for whom they are responsible – feeding, cleaning and changing them. It seems that it is not humanly possible for them to form close emotional relationships with so many young children without suffering from emotional overload; so they have to retreat to the safer areas of caring for the children's physical needs. In the hustle and bustle of getting through the daily tasks involved in the physical care of the children for whom they are responsible, staff are not able to use the kind of enriching, affectionate talk around these routines which, Bruner argued, forms the basis of babies' learning about 'conversations'.

Learning to love books

While Ivy focused on speaking and listening, Jenny was interested in the effects of introducing babies to books. She was influenced by the work of Barrie Wade (1993) in the Bookstart Scheme who monitored the impact of giving books to babies and supporting their parents in story reading skills. His seminal work was extended nationally by the Book Trust (Book Trust 1998).

Jenny's professional role was to support family literacy in a local authority funded project. She based her action research cycles on work with mother and toddler groups meeting in primary schools, clinics or community centres. Over 40 parents or carers were contacted via health visitors and given a bookbag when their babies were 7 months old. The bookbag contained: a board book, some simple advice about books, a library joining card and times of the local library sessions, a song and rhyme booklet, a poster and a bookmark. The pack also included an invitation for parents to join a series of workshops to help their babies' literacy development. A third of those contacted took up the offer of attending the workshops. They were from a wide range of socioeconomic and educational backgrounds. The only thing they had in common was a baby aged 7 months!

Each workshop, held once a fortnight, had a focus but, as with Ivy's work with parents, allowed time for socialization. For many isolated parents, the chance to socialize during the day was a very important benefit of attending the workshops. There was always a crèche worker to help look after the babies; but mostly the babies just clambered around amongst the adults. Jenny was the first to admit that some of her workshops worked better than others: *'Indeed, the occasional session was chaotic as I tried, unsuccessfully, to compete with up to twelve extremely vocal and mobile babies! However, we had a lot of fun at the sessions too.'*

The content of the workshops was geared around the needs and ideas of each particular group of parents or carers, but a typical menu would be: how to share books with babies; choosing books for babies; songs and rhymes; making books; early language development; promoting literacy skills at home; drawing and writing; learning to read; encouraging speaking and listening skills; television. There were always plenty of books around for the babies and adults to enjoy together, and the opportunity to take a book home for the fortnight. Parents were asked to notice which books their babies liked best – the format (board or cloth), the layout (with text or without; photos or illustrations), and the content (stories they enjoyed). Jenny was fascinated to observe the definite preferences of the babies for types of books or for particular transitory favourites. Their likes and dislikes seemed to be based on a combination of features – preferences for the feel of board books or cloth books, the impact of photo illustrations rather than drawings, the connections images made with important objects in their own lives, the kinds of fun interactions the books induced in their parents or carers. She observed that the babies quickly learned how to hold the books and turn the pages once book behaviours had been modelled by the adults sharing books with them and were capable of concentrating on books for short periods on their own.

Using the knowledge they had gained of what their babies most enjoyed, the parents or carers were given the opportunity to choose a second book for their babies when they reached 12 months.

Jenny's notes identified changes in the parents' behaviours too:

> It was pleasing to observe the parents' surprise and joy at what, with a little encouragement from them, their babies were actually achieving. For the majority of parents this was like an awakening. 'I didn't know my baby would be able to do this. What else can she do?' From the original impetus of the workshops, groups of parents are continuing to meet to look at how babies develop through play. The parents are 'hooked'. They also enjoyed the social side of meeting. Role modeling of parenting skills within the groups has had a strong impact. It has made me review the way I work to 'spread the word' about the development of literacy in babies.

In her evaluation of her work for the project, Jenny noted:

> Observing the literacy behaviour of both the parents and their babies was a fascinating and very satisfying experience as I watched the changes in both. The really exciting thing was that we, the parents and I, actually saw the babies taking a keen interest in, and responding enthusiastically to, books. As the parents became more confident, the parent/baby interaction around the books blossomed and we saw a love of books being fostered in the babies.

We will return to a more detailed discussion about the key principles of involving parents in young children's development and learning in Chapter 9.

18 months to 3 years

Mark-making

Val has a teaching background. At the time of the project she was employed on a local authority scheme with the dual aims of helping parents/carers to learn more about their children's education while at the same time encouraging them to further their own learning through training or employment opportunities. She was supporting a literacy programme through a weekly parent and toddler club which had been running for two and a half years in a classroom at a primary school.

She noticed that there were less opportunities for the toddlers to explore mark-making than other aspects of literacy. Each week pencils, crayons and paper were set out on a table, but she noted that the children spent little time there, and parents even less. She decided to make mark-making, drawing and emergent writing the focus of her research. She began to read around the subject and noted in her diary: *'Although I had worked within an early years framework for over ten years, when I carried out a literature search and review of emergent writing there was still a lot I didn't know and needed to find out. I was not an expert.'*

Val planned a sequence of activities with a specific focus each week on strategies to encourage mark-making and writing skills. The target areas were listed as: hand-eye coordination, fine motor control, experimenting with a range of media, teaching the vocabulary of drawing and emergent writing, and extending children's learning.

Once she got going she observed that while she was seated at the table children came willingly to join in with the activities, appeared to enjoy them and were making progress in the skills targeted. But despite her years of experience as a teacher, she confessed that she found it a challenge to judge exactly when to extend, challenge or direct such young children's mark-making. Entries from her diary show just how much the children, aged from 11 to 36 months, were learning about drawing and writing:

> Ellie, aged 11 months, moved towards the crayons, picked them up and began to explore them one by one with her mouth. She watched what the other children were doing, moved away but came back to the table several more times.

Damien, aged 2 years and 4 months, indicated that he wanted to use the pencil I was holding to draw. He said, 'Pencil draw'. I offered him a variety of pencils and chubby crayons from the pot. Damien chose the pencils. He made several spiral patterns.

Katy, aged 2 years and 11 months, had good pencil control. She drew me a number of star shapes and a traveling zigzag pattern. I chatted with her about what she was doing and she repeated that she had drawn a zigzag picture. I was making notes and Katy asked me what I was doing. I explained that I was writing about her drawing. She asked me why and I said that I thought that it was interesting and that she was good at drawing. She asked me to write her name, first on my page and then on her piece of paper. She made some marks on her paper, pushed it across to show me and told me she'd written her name.

Alice, aged 3 years, drew several rectangular shapes on her paper and told me they were fences. She also made several marks and then began to copy letters in her name – A and C. The letters were well formed and she managed to match them accurately to the letters I'd written. I praised her and pointed out the similarities between other marks she'd been making and the letters in her name.

In her research diary Val noted that she believed that the parents were not engaging with what she was doing with the children on the mark-making table. She wrote: *'At first I thought I had created a cocoon around children's learning and essentially left parents outside it. However, closer observations revealed that many of the parents were listening and observing the interactions that were taking place.'* She then made the strategic decision to mount a display of the children's mark-making and emergent writing for the parents on the board in the classroom where the parent and toddler club met. She was staggered by its impact on the parents: *'The display became an amazing tool through which to discuss the children's writing/drawing development. I pointed out to them recurring patterns, movements or the beginning of letter shapes, representational drawings or invented writing.'*

In Bruner's (1996) terms the display board became a cultural tool around which a series of interactions between the children, their parents and the practitioners, situated in the context of the parent and toddler club workshops, focused on the children's understanding of how to make meanings in drawing and writing (see Chapter 4 for discussion about the way in which children are inducted to be competent users of the cultural tools of society). However, there were too many drawing/ writing examples being generated to display them all, so Val suggested that each parent might like to use an exercise book to mount and display their own children's work as a way of monitoring their progress over the weeks. The parents brought in photographs of the children to stick on the front of the exercise books. The books became a focus for the parent and child to review what they had been doing each week as they stuck in their drawings and mark-making. Once again a simple exercise book became a cultural tool in the process of creating shared understandings between parents and professionals. Val noted in her research diary: *'The eagerness of the parents to stick the children's work into the books and record their descriptions of how they'd been arrived at really took me by surprise.'* The parents began to understand the subtlety and power of young children's mark-making. One parent remarked to Val: 'I used to think it was just scribbling.'

For the next step of her research, Val decided to move on to encouraging parents and children to make connections between their own mark-making and written communication in the real world. She knew that the local post office was a regular port of call for parents on their way to and from the school. She asked the parents to lift the children up when they next visited the post office so that they could see what was going on over the counter. She encouraged them to talk to the children during the week about writing and posting letters, paying bills, buying stamps, weighing parcels, cashing giros etc. At the next workshop session she launched the idea of making a role-play area for the children based on the post office. Over the next few weeks the parents collected resources – junk mail, postcards, envelopes, stamps, forms, greetings cards – and made equipment, a post box and a counter, for the toddlers' post office. Parents were relaxed about joining the children in the role-play where the stimulus for talk and play was a real shared experience. Adults and children wrote, drew, filled in forms, talked about symbols and logos and filled in lottery tickets together. One of the children persuaded her mother to set up a sub-post office at home!

Several of the parents began to notice how closely the children watched when they were writing. One said to Val: 'He often wants to write himself now when he sees me writing.' Adults were drawn quite naturally into extending the children's knowledge base without recourse to mimicking didactic teaching styles. It was suddenly OK for parents and children to write and draw together companionably in joint involvement episodes with both adults and children paying respectful attention to each other's meaning making. Val noted one parent carefully explaining the concept of a prepaid envelope to her 3-year-old.

In her evaluation of what she had learned from her research, Val wrote: *'We learnt how important it was to tune into and discuss with children their drawings and emergent writing as they were doing it and to encourage further efforts by giving feedback and showing real interest in their mark-making.'*

Kress (1997: 17) made the same important point about paying serious attention to children's mark-making:

> The child's written signs are the effect of their meaning-making actions, arising out of their interest, using what they have available as representational means ... The signs which children make are, despite their differences from adult form, fully meaningful in every sense. The child's actions have to be understood as productive and transformative of their own representational resources, as well as those of the community around them.

For Val, another important self-realization was that by adopting the 'school' behaviours of sitting and 'teaching' children at the 'work table' she had inadvertently excluded the parents from engaging with their children. Once she had demystified 'the mark-making table' by letting parents into the magic circle of 'teacher' knowledge by literally 'displaying' it to them on the notice board, and interpreting that explanation in terms that made sense to her audience, they became hooked on their own personal journeys of discovery about the meanings their own children were making in marks.

It is this kind of approach that makes the philosophy of the famous Reggio Emilia pre-school centres so compelling (Edwards *et al.* 1993). Pedagogues, practitioners, parents and children are engaged together in exploring the many languages children use to express their ideas and communicate their meaning making to others. Malaguzzi (1987), the founding father of the Reggio Emilia pre-school innovation, argued that 'our image of the child should be of one that is rich in potential, strong, powerful, competent and most of all connected to adults and other children'. In this example of a reflective practitioner at work, children, practitioners and parents were empowered by acknowledging the central role of learning associated with the language of their everyday lives within their knowledge community. Most importantly, children, parents and professionals were learning from and about each other.

3 to 5 years

From 2- to 3-D representation and back again

Molly was the manager of an inner-city early years centre. The staff had been working for some time to enhance the quality of mark-making across all areas of the curriculum, but they had noticed that it was rare to observe children's mark-making being connected to play in the construction area. They had also observed that the range of children regularly using the construction area during free-flow times in the mornings was limited. Boys dominated construction play. Access in the afternoons was restricted by the fact that the resources were housed in a 'family base' where children were based with their key-worker.

Molly identified the focus of her action research cycle as the promotion of meaning making in construction play for the 3- to 5-year-olds. Her aims were: to increase access to construction play for more children; to encourage the use of mark-making in the construction area; to improve the quality of interactions between adults and children in the construction area; to extend children's learning through 2-D representations and 3-D models in meaning making.

Molly set out an action plan that involved the staff recording their own observations of activities in the construction area in an agreed format. The format was a simple chart with spaces to record the name, gender and age of the child observed; other children with whom they played; whether an adult was involved; what the children did; language used and any evidence of mark-making in general or specifically related to construction activities. The first sets of observations were gathered during the month of October. Molly and her deputy also made some observations in the area. Molly noted that though the staff were slightly uncomfortable at first about being observed they quickly forgot she was there.

When the first set of staff observations were analysed and the results shared at a staff meeting several key issues were raised. The most usual number of children working together was three. Boys represented two-thirds of the children using the area. In half of the observations children were not talking. One-third of the observations showed children using mark-making, but only 5 per cent of these were linked to construction play. It tended to be the same children who regularly played in the area.

However, the analysis of activities observed when Molly and her deputy were observing the area later in the month showed quite different patterns. In these, the girls represented two-thirds and the boys one-third of those actively involved in construction play. Language and mark-making related to construction was much more apparent. As Molly ruefully observed, the effect of the managers' presence in the area clearly had a dramatic impact on how the practitioners structured their own and the children's participation!

As the project progressed it became clear that the staff were unsure about how to get the best out of meaning making through construction play. Molly set up a series of visits to other pre-school settings for staff to observe the quality of their construction activities. She invited one of the researchers to give an input at a staff meeting followed by a workshop for staff to explore the possibilities for themselves of construction materials (Community Playthings, Duplo, Mobilo, H. Blocks and Stickle Bricks) and small figure play. In a second session they were encouraged to use drawing or writing to extend their thinking. Staff were asked to use these experiences as the basis for planning a series of activities for the children.

In December the staff and Molly set about a second set of observations in the construction area to monitor for any changes. For Molly there were some disappointments: boys still dominated two-thirds of the activities and there was evidence that the same rather limited range of children were playing in the area. However, there was a dramatic increase in the amount of mark-making related to the construction play to 85 per cent of the incidents. Overall, children used mark-making in the area for two-thirds of the time they were observed.

A typical observation involved the follow-up activity of the story of *Goldilocks and the Three Bears*. In the construction area the staff had collected together several copies of the story, Community Plaything blocks, paper, card, scissors, glue sticks and felt-tip pens. The observation recorded how the children moved frequently backwards and forwards between making the chairs, tables and beds out of the blocks and role playing the story, taking turns to play the main characters; drawing out props such as the porridge bowls and spoons on big sheets of paper and cutting them out to use in play episodes; and then making small pictures of the bears and Goldilocks on the card and cutting them out to play a second version of the story in miniature. Finally, these second-level representations were stuck together with sellotape onto a base board cut from an old cardboard box to recreate the story scene in an elaborate and detailed model. Molly noted in her diary:

> The adults learned how children have the ability to recall from a previous day and transfer a story into representations in the construction area taking one step further each time. They also learned that children are good role models for each other in sparking off ideas about expressing themselves in speech, 3-D models and 2-D drawings.

Molly's project was a wonderful example of Kress's (1997) and Pahl's (1999) multi-modal representations, and of children using Bruner's (1996) enactive and iconic representations. With its emphasis on both language and mathematical thinking, it is a good point at which to move on to the chapters on how young children learn to become mathematicians.

Suggested reading

For prompts for nursery rhymes and action songs the old but well-tried Matterson, E. (1969) *This Little Puffin: Finger Play and Nursery Rhymes* (London: Puffin) is a good collection. Raymond Briggs's *The Mother Goose Treasury* (1969), published by Hamish Hamilton and Puffin is a good anthology of nursery rhymes. The Opies' *Children's Games in Street and Playground*, published by Oxford University Press in 1969 is a useful source of information on traditional street and playground games.

Further reading on the emotional aspects of learning includes Daniel Golman's (1996) *Emotional Intelligence* published by Bloomsbury and Marion Dowling's second edition (2005) of *Young Children's Personal, Social and Emotional Development*, published by Paul Chapman Publishing.

Leila Berg's (1977) *Reading and Loving*, published by Routledge & Kegan Paul, is a classic. She describes the warmth and sensuous delights of young children sharing the enjoyment of learning to read with caring adults. Vivian Paley's *A Child's Work* published in 2004 by University of Chicago Press explores the role of dramatic play as an essential tool for exploring the social and emotional world of young children.

7   Mathematical learning

Becoming a numerate person

Is being numerate simply a question of being good with numbers? The 1982 Cockcroft Report, which has had an enormous influence on mathematics education, suggests that being numerate implies:

> the possession of two attributes. The first is an 'at-homeness' with numbers and an ability to cope with the practical mathematical demands of everyday life. The second is an ability to have some appreciation and understanding of information which is presented in mathematical terms, for instance in graphs, charts or tables ... a numerate person should be able to appreciate and understand some of the ways in which mathematics can be used as a means of communication. (Cockcroft 1982: para. 34)

Being numerate, therefore, is more than a recognition of numbers, is closely linked to mathematical understandings and serves two purposes. First, numeracy is useful in everyday life and second, it allows us to think mathematically in specifically mathematical contexts.

'At-homeness' with numbers is certainly important. Research over the last two decades has been telling us that familiarity with numbers and their uses helps children to think mathematically (Nunes and Bryant 1996). This may seem so obvious that it is not worth mentioning. However, so strong has been the influence of Piaget and his concern with children learning through action rather than through language, that pre-school provision has often emphasized sorting and matching at the expense of number. Munn and Schaffer (1993), for example, in their detailed study of literacy and numeracy interactions in Strathclyde nurseries in the early 1990s found a surprisingly low level of numeracy-based interactions between children and adults.

Our research partnership worked with the messages from research about the need to offer a developmentally sound set of experiences to children to support early numeracy slowly and carefully, and to provide opportunities for children to use their developing mathematical understandings. Our thinking about children and mathematics took us, usually simultaneously, to three focuses: young children as mathematical thinkers, how adults support children's mathematical thinking and the mathematical experiences that can be provided in pre-school settings. In this chapter we shall look at young children as mathematical thinkers. In the next chapter we shall examine how early education settings can support children's mathematical thinking and will illustrate the discussion with examples of provision from the partnership.

Young children as mathematical thinkers

Being able to think mathematically

Children learn a great deal about aspects of mathematics before they start formal school (Aubrey 1996). They therefore enter school with a great deal of knowledge on which teachers can build. But then something seems to go wrong. Very few students specialize in mathematics beyond A level and a large number leave school disliking mathematics. Current thinking suggests that the problem lies in seeing mathematics as a set of formal principles that are learnt as abstract knowledge and then applied in the world. People are simply not very good at applying abstract principles to real life situations.

As a result, efforts have been made to ensure that we help children to learn mathematical principles in situations that are as near to real life as possible (De Corte *et al.* 1996). The rationale is that when they deal with real life mathematical problems children learn mathematical principles, develop a disposition to engage with mathematics and learn useful mathematics which they can use in both everyday life and in more formal mathematics situations. Early education settings are well placed to work with this view of mathematics as situated in real life settings, as thankfully they are not constrained by a history of mathematics teaching that emphasizes abstract problem solving. In pre-school settings children can gradually learn to operate mathematically in situations that are part of their general exploration of their worlds.

However, in order to be able to operate mathematically in an activity a child needs to recognize the mathematics in the experience, be able to think logically about the response and have the strategies available to be able to respond. Children's understanding of basic logical concepts is therefore central to how they see, interpret and respond to activities that can be tackled mathematically. We can't do justice here to Piaget's work on children's logico-mathematical thought and the frameworks which have drawn on it (see, for example, Campbell and Olson 1990; Meadows

1993). Equally, however, we cannot discuss mathematical thinking without mentioning *conservation*.

Conservation of quantity in Piaget's writings refers to a child's capacity to know that the quantity remains the same even though its shape may be changed. For example, conservation of continuous quantity is achieved when children recognize that when a ball of Plasticine is rolled into a sausage or when the water from a squat beaker is poured into a tall narrow one, the quantities in each case are not changed. *Conservation of number* is evident when children can tell that a set of objects – for example, five sweets – remains a set of five sweets whether they are arrayed in a line or in a circle. Conservation of number is particularly important for the development of numeracy as we shall see when we discuss cardinal numbers in a moment.

Children's mathematical development is therefore a complex interplay between how they interpret their worlds and how they are able to respond to what they understand. The challenge that their mathematical learning presents to early educators is perhaps greater than children's literacy development because the mathematics in children's worlds is less obviously evident to them. We therefore need to think carefully about how we elicit the mathematics in children's experiences and give them the wherewithal to deal with it. We do know that an understanding of number helps children to respond mathematically so we shall make this our first focus.

The development of children's understanding of number

In Chapter 4 we suggested that adults should think aloud so that children can begin to glimpse how they see, interpret and respond to the world. Children can then appropriate adults' responses. Let's listen to a mother thinking aloud while waiting for a number Seven bus with her 4-year-old: 'Oh dear that's the third Fifty Three in the last five minutes! Even if a Seven comes now we'll be a couple of minutes late. Oh here it is! Have you got your two ten pences ready?'

The mother's talk is rich in number but it also tells us just how difficult it is to understand numbers. She has used number in a variety of ways: to *denote* (i.e. 'a [number] Seven'); to *order* (i.e. 'the third'); and to indicate a *number in a set* (i.e. 'two'). This is without the complications of large numbers, time, money and alternative language such as 'a couple'. Children may appropriate the language – that is, learn language formats such as 'one for you and one for me' or 'none left' – but do not so quickly grasp the meanings. Learning to use the language of number and to become numerate is a complex process and *takes a very long time*.

Children are immersed in numerical experiences in their daily lives whether they are being persuaded to eat 'one more' spoonful of yoghurt or having their feet measured for shoes. However, it is clear that even though young children can respond to these activities in conversations with adults, they do not understand the numbers involved in the same ways that adults do. This lack of understanding is hardly surprising when we consider the different ways that numbers are used. Fuson and Hall (1983) suggest that young children meet number words in at least six different contexts and in each they serve a slightly different purpose:

1. In the *sequence context*, strings of numbers are produced in the conventional order but there is no intention to count objects. For example: 'One, two, three, four, five. Once I caught a fish alive.' Or, 'Close your eyes and count to ten.'
2. In the *counting context*, numbers are applied to objects. For example, by pointing to or touching objects as they are counted.
3. In the *cardinal context*, numbers represent what Fuson and Hall describe as the 'manyness' or numerosity of a set of objects. The ability to use number in this way comes gradually – for example, children understand 'two' quite early through familiarity with two shoes, two gloves etc. Young children also learn, through stories, that there are three bears and three Billy Goats Gruff. But recognizing the cardinal qualities of a number – that is, actually understanding that the last number you say when counting a set of objects represents the number of objects in the set, comes relatively slowly and depends on a child's capacity to *conserve* numbers.
4. In the *measure context*, number words represent the manyness or numerosity of the units of measurement used. In the construction area in Alison's centre Connor demonstrated his early gropings towards understanding linear measurement when, after applying the tape measure to his boat, he told Alison that it measured '150,000 pounds'.
5. In the *ordinal context*, a number word represents the relative position, size or other measurable of an object in a group of objects (the third bus to pass the stop, the second tallest person in the group or the fourth child in the family).
6. In the *nonnumerical context*, number words are simply names – for example, a number Seven bus, the number of your house, a telephone number. Fuson and Hall suggest that too much attention to nonnumerical numbers might inhibit children's understandings of the other qualities of numbers.

In addition to distinguishing the different uses of numbers in different contexts children need to understand some basic principles about counting before they can be said to be able to count. Gelman and Gallistel (1986) identified five such principles:

1. The *one-to-one principle* requires children to be able to match the counting words to the items to be counted.
2. The *stable order principle* refers to children's ability to repeat counting words in the correct order. This is particularly demanding in the English language which has less of a stable pattern in its number words compared with some other languages. Children therefore need to learn number sequences by rote in the first instance.
3. The *cardinal principle* has already been described. Grasping this principle is central to a child's capacity to add or subtract.
4. The *abstraction principle* alerts us to the fact that children do not need to count sets of similar objects in order to use cardinal numbers. That is, they do not need to count four cups to label the collection as a set of four. They will, for example, be able to label sets of 'things on the table' as four 'things'.
5. The *order irrelevance principle* is evident when children can happily start to count a set of objects from any point in the set. That is, they are recognizing that an object is not a 'one' but that numbers are used simply to count and not to label individual objects.

The interplay between first recognizing the mathematics in a situation and then using and developing mathematical responses is quite messy. Saxe *et al.* explored the relationship between numerical 'function' (what numbers are used for – e.g. indicating the total number in a set, comparing sets) and the 'forms' of numerical activity undertaken by young children (the strategies children use when they tackle a mathematical function – e.g. counting, one-to-one matching). As part of their study of parents, children between the ages of 30 and 60 months and numeracy, they came up with a developmental sequence showing the relationship between the mathematics in an activity and the strategies children use to deal with number experiences. The sequence has four levels with Level 1 as the least complex (Saxe *et al.* 1987: 8–12). We have illustrated their sequence with our own examples, as follows.

At *Level 1*, children use number words without making a lasting one-to-one match between a word and an object. They will produce a sequence of numbers, though not necessarily in the correct order and will not appear to use numbers to represent the manyness or cardinal aspect of a set of objects. For example, when faced with five sweets to count children may point vaguely and say one, two, three, six, eight. Or, having counted the sweets correctly to five, they will recount when asked how many sweets there are.

At *Level 2*, children can match a number to an object and can therefore count objects. Furthermore, they recognize that the last number they said represents the number of objects in the set they have counted. For example, having counted the five sweets in front of them they can tell you that there are five sweets on the table – that is, they can *conserve* numbers and use them as cardinal numbers.

At *Level 3*, children can compare two groups of numbers and can reproduce a second set of numbers. But they do so by using the counting strategies they used at Level 2. For example, they will compare two sets of sweets by one-to-one matching. They will not count to five and then to four and say that the first set has one more sweet.

At *Level 4*, children begin to use arithmetic strategies. For example, when asked to add two sets of numbers they will start with the cardinal number of the first set (five sweets) and count on the four in the second set as six, seven, eight, nine.

Children's understanding of number seems to develop slowly and build on previous experiences. Even babies appear to recognize the difference between sets of two and of three objects (Baroody 1987) and 2-year-olds start to string together number sequences even though they may not be counting as they do so. It is also clear from the four levels just outlined that as children move through the levels of competence they build directly on their achievements at the previous level. Saxe *et al.* (1987) suggested that children pass through these levels aided by adults who help them to use their existing numerical skills to tackle slightly more complex problems and develop new understandings. For example, once a child understands that if four people are to sit at the table four places need to be set (a Level 2 understanding), she or he can be encouraged to collect sets of four forks, knives, plates etc. (leading to a Level 3 understanding). Importantly, children tackle these problems in activities that are embedded, often playfully, in conversations and games. These conversations and games provide children with familiar language and action formats which enable them to safely explore the mathematical challenges that are offered.

The distinction outlined by Saxe *et al.* (1987) between mathematical demands in an activity and the strategies that children bring to bear on them is helpful for two reasons. First, it tells us that adults can help children identify the potential mathematics in an activity. Second, it reminds us to build on children's current strategies when first tackling a new mathematical experience. A nice example of how adults can build on children's current understandings to extend their mathematical thinking is found in a study by Muldoon, Lewis and Freeman (2003). In their study with 4-year-olds they discovered that although the ability to count was necessary if children were to be able to create matching sets, the best predictor of success at the task was the ability to identify and reason about someone else's miscounts. That is, the children were able to represent in their talk the rules of cardinality. The research team concluded that early education should include the opportunity to judge and discuss the counting proficiency of others.

It is clear from the outlines of number contexts and uses we have given, that children's abilities simply to reproduce number words tells us very little about how they understand number and what it is that they believe numbers are and do. Penny Munn's interviews and assessments with 4-year-old children in Strathclyde pre-school settings in the year before formal schooling revealed that although the children were able to sequence numbers very well, they had little sense of number as a way of quantifying – rather, they saw it as something playful (Munn 1997a). Munn suggests that although the children appeared to be counting they were not doing so as a mathematical activity but as an imitative activity. We have already suggested in Chapter 4 that imitation of behaviour and appropriation of language are important features of learning. However, they are not the same as mastery, and Munn's observations remind us of the need for careful assessment before moving children on to more demanding number activities.

Clearly, children's early familiarity with number words and how they are used appears to be beneficial. If using numbers is associated with fun and achievement in playful number activities children are being helped to acquire a disposition to deal with numbers and sets of behaviours, such as pointing and sequencing, that will give them confidence. Also, once children have some number vocabulary they can use it when exploring patterns, sorting shapes, weighing objects or assessing capacity, and therefore more widely interpret and respond to the mathematics around them.

Importantly, a developing understanding of number and its uses leads children towards the recording of their experiences through mark-making, which gradually becomes more systematic and again assists their mathematical thinking.

Learning to record

Cockcroft's (1982) definition of being numerate given at the beginning of this chapter describes mathematics as a means of communication. We would argue that being able to communicate mathematically is valuable in both daily life and in specifically mathematical contexts such as formal schooling. Sometimes that communication is with others and sometimes with ourselves when we make mathematical records in order to assist our own problem solving.

However, in order to communicate mathematically, young learners need first to recognize that there is a connection between the mark that they make and what it stands for – for example, that one splodge in a circle stands for one person at the tea table. Only gradually will young children learn to convert their own private and situation-specific system of signs into a system that is context-free and easily understood by others. The first step, that a mark represents a quantity, is therefore important. But all that we have said about number suggests that this ability is quite an achievement for a young child and appears to develop gradually alongside a growing understanding of how numbers are used and of the publicly understood numeral system.

Munn (1994b) identified six ways in which children record numbers after 'counting' which seem to indicate children's developing ability to use numbers as symbols (that is, understanding that the numeral '4' represents a cardinal number). Children's recording strategies range from 'pretend writing' to 'conventionally used numerals' and are shown in Figure 7.1.

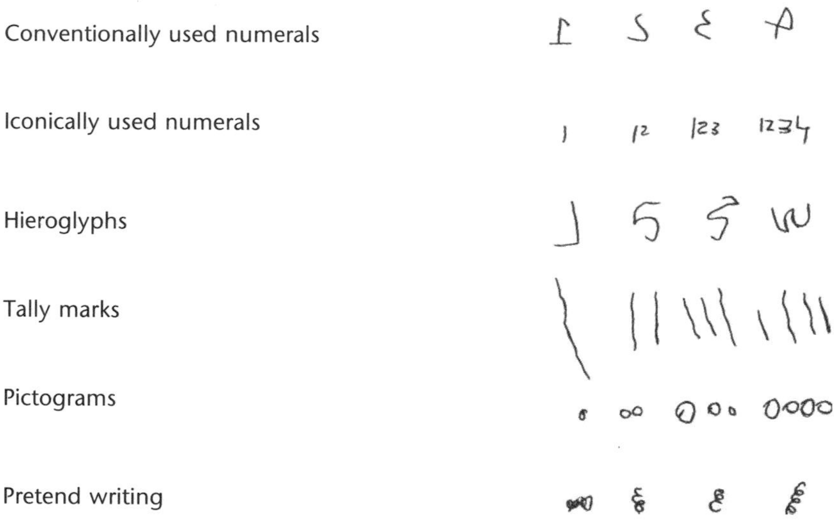

Conventionally used numerals

Iconically used numerals

Hieroglyphs

Tally marks

Pictograms

Pretend writing

Figure 7.1 Children's recording strategies in number
Source: Munn (1994b).

After monitoring the development in recording and the strategic use of number of 49 children in their final year before starting school, Munn (1997b) concluded that children's ability to read their own number records, regardless of whether these were recorded as numerals, seems to support and be supported by their developing understanding of number and its uses.

Munn's conclusions (1997b) about the relationships between children's strategies and their numerical thinking once again remind us of the complex relationship between use of numbers and mathematical understanding outlined by Saxe *et al.* (1987). One challenge to early educators arising from Munn's conclusions is: just how do we pace children's recording and ensure that children's representations of number assist them to use number? We cannot help children to understand what numbers are and do simply by training them to write the number symbols. For example, when Munn assessed the same children after one term of formal schooling (Munn 1997b), she found that seven of the children who had learnt to write numerals while at formal school were not referring to the numbers they had written to help them answer her questions. It seemed that they had learnt how to form the numerals but not how to use them strategically as numbers when faced with a mathematical activity.

Munn's work suggests that being able to use and understand numerals helps children once they need to be able to refer to their written records to support their mathematical problem solving. She therefore advises early years professionals to be alert to children's developing number 'literacy' (Munn 1997b). However, Munn's point about number literacy is a subtle but important one. She argues that developing number literacy cannot be seen as similar to emergent writing. This is because children's meaningful use of numerals depends on their understanding of the number concept being represented by the numeral – for example, that 'five' is being used in a particular situation as a cardinal number. Munn's analysis is supported by other researchers working in the field of young children's early mathematical learning (Baroody 1993). Pre-school teachers therefore have to guard against introducing numerals too rapidly.

Before they achieve number literacy children can be helped by adults who talk to them about their alternative symbols in ways that encourage them to understand how their tallies or drawings do represent specific quantities and how these representations can act as records of their counting. These interactions should occur as part of open-ended activities which allow children to construct their own understandings of numbers and how they can be used so that they can move, over time, to use numbers when they record. This case is also made strongly by

Dijk, van Oers and Terwel (2004) who argue that children's representations ('schematisations' or 'perceptual models') form the 'bridge between the concrete practical thinking of young children and the logical-symbolic thinking in later development'. They also argue, like Munn, that it is important to help children to discuss their representations and to reinforce the communicative qualities of mathematics which help make mathematical thinking meaningful.

The range of mathematical experiences in pre-school provision

In this chapter we have focused largely, though not entirely, on number. This is because it seems clear that a grasp of basic numeracy concepts helps children as they think and act as young mathematicians while operating in their worlds whether they are, for example, measuring, weighing or sorting. However, early mathematics is not simply a question of understanding numbers and how they are used. Mathematical activities include becoming familiar with shapes, learning to recognize patterns, working with ordering and sequencing, and planning and problem solving.

All of these experiences are easily incorporated into fun activities for children. We cannot overestimate the importance of mathematics as fun in early education. Like Dijk and her colleagues in their work on developmental education in the Netherlands (van Oers 1996, 1999), we are influenced by Vygotskian understandings of learning and development. We therefore recognize, as Vygotsky did, that for young children, play is the 'leading activity'. When we discussed the idea of a leading activity in Chapter 4 we described it as the social situation most likely to contribute to the development of new ways of thinking and acting. For young children, the leading activity is play and opportunities for learning need to be embedded in play.

For example, sequencing and pattern recognition can become part of printing or painting activities. Becoming familiar with shapes is often part of dance and song times, and, of course, cooking and eating. Sequencing is a central aspect of stories whether children listen or are encouraged to tell or act out their own short narratives. Ordering is experienced at meal times, in singing, and everyday turn-taking. Sorting and set making are often parts of tidy-up routines. Planning and problem solving can be encouraged in building and role-play.

As we shall see in the next chapter our research partners were inventive in how they ensured that mathematical focuses could be found in role-play, imaginative games, songs and other familiar pre-school contexts. The children were able to engage with the mathematics, sometimes with the help of adults who modelled language and behaviour in conversations, and sometimes simply because the resources captured children's imaginations and led them to particular forms of behaviour.

Building on children's everyday experiences of mathematics

We have stressed that children's experience in pre-school settings is not a question of simply preparing children for the school curriculum. Rather it is an opportunity to develop young children's cultural capital so that they enter school as keen learners with a strong sense of their own effectiveness and with some of the basic conceptual understandings on which more formal forms of schooling can build. Far more than schools, pre-school settings are able to work closely with parents and collaborate over the informal learning experiences that are part of the cultural capital provided at home.

As we have already seen in this chapter the informal learning and cultural capital provided at home in mathematics can be considerable (Aubrey *et al.* 2003; Baroody 2000). One of the challenges facing teachers in the first few years of formal schooling is how to translate informal understandings, which are sometimes of limited use in formal mathematics, into more accepted ways of thinking and acting mathematically. This challenge will not face many early education practitioners; for them the emphasis has to be on developing and augmenting the everyday mathematical experiences of young children so that they familiarize themselves with mathematical concepts that are embedded in meaningful experiences. We also suggest that these meaningful experiences are not necessarily domestic experiences. We agree with Gifford (2004) that the domesticating of number to keep it close to everyday life is not a helpful way forward. First, one cannot make assumptions about the practices to be found in children's homes in culturally diverse societies. Second, children's experience of number is increasingly through technology and there is a great deal of prior knowledge to be built on in that area.

The focus in pre-school mathematics is therefore a question of developing children's enthusiastic dispositions towards seeing the mathematics in situations and having the mathematical knowledge on which to draw in order to respond. The role of the assisting adult is therefore to sustain motivation, to help children see the mathematics and to offer some aids to organizing their responses, perhaps by modelling – for example, seeing patterns, sorting into sets, or using cardinal numbers when describing sets.

In order to help children develop as mathematical thinkers, adults need to understand how children are interpreting the mathematical potential in the experience and understand how they can help children see a little more of the mathematics available. As Saxe *et al.* (1987) suggest in the area of numeracy, this is done by helping children see how mathematics can be used in the situation and then by helping them develop the strategies they need to engage with the mathematics.

Figure 7.2 can help us see what is happening when young children encounter mathematical experiences. We can see from Figure 7.2 that adults have to make two analyses if they are to enhance the mathematics in a child's experience. They have to recognize the mathematical potential themselves and they have to interpret how the child is also likely to experience it. They then use these analyses to make judgements about how they might help the child see a little more of the mathematics and use or develop the wherewithal to deal mathematically with what they see. Having made these judgements adults then make pedagogical decisions about how to help children to see and respond. Adults help by

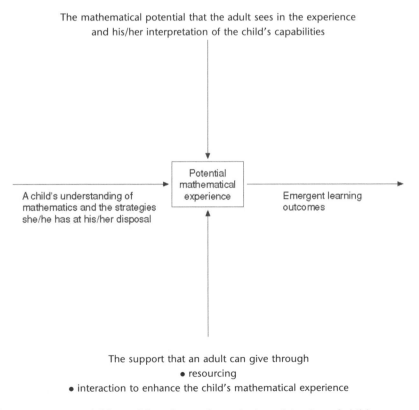

Figure 7.2 A model for guiding the mathematical participation of children

providing particular resources and interacting with children in specific ways. The learning outcomes for children that emerge from mathematical experiences will depend, in part at least, on how adults manage the support that they provide so that a child can participate mathematically in an experience that has mathematical potential. We shall turn to these issues in the next chapter.

However, we shall conclude this chapter by emphasizing the need to help children develop positive dispositions towards mathematics and to do that through a wide variety of enjoyable experiences. De Corte *et al.* (1996: 508), in their comprehensive review of mathematics teaching and learning, talk of developing feelings, sensitivity and inclinations to engage with mathematical opportunities, and of the need for learners to experience mathematics in range of activities: 'the disposition cannot be directly taught but has to develop over an extended period of time; this implies that the organization of teaching cannot be restricted to a set of discrete goals.'

The comment refers to the learning of mathematics throughout life but is particularly true, we suggest, when thinking about very young children. For early mathematics the lessons from research in mathematics education are that:

- mathematical understanding develops slowly;
- new understandings build on earlier ones so stages cannot be jumped;
- children need a wide range of mathematical experiences;
- mathematical experiences need to be meaningfully embedded in enjoyable activities;
- a disposition to engage with mathematics is crucial;
- adults can help through careful monitoring and by providing conversational support.

The message for early education professionals is, therefore, that children cannot be rushed into performing mathematically. We need to pay attention to how children are making sense of the mathematics around them and encourage them to enjoy thinking mathematically.

Suggested reading

Thompson, I. (ed.) (1997) *Teaching and Learning Early Number* (Buckingham: Open University Press) remains an excellent collection of papers on current research on young children and number.

The classic collection of papers on children's thinking and mathematics remains Ginsburg, H. (ed.) (1983) *The Development of Mathematical Thinking* (New York: Academic Press).

A wide-ranging and highly informative review of current research on teaching and learning in mathematics is De Corte, E., Greer, B. and Verschaffel, L. (1996) 'Mathematics teaching and learning', in D. Berliner and R. Calfee (eds) *Handbook of Educational Psychology* (New York: Macmillan).

If you are interested in the ideas on culture and becoming a mathematical thinker we have been discussing you may like to explore these issues more generally through research on mathematics teaching in schools. Seeger, F., Voigt, J. and Waschescio, U. (eds) (1998) *The Culture of the Mathematics Classroom* (Cambridge: Cambridge University Press) is an interesting collection of papers on sociocultural approaches to the learning of mathematics.

A useful review of research on computers in early mathematics education by Douglas Clements echoes much of what we have been saying about not underestimating children's capacity for thinking and acting mathematically and usefully augments our discussions and the points made by Gifford on young children, mathematical experience and technology. Published in 2002 in *Contemporary Issues in Early Childhood* 3 (1), pp. 160–81, it is entitled Computers in Early Childhood Mathematics.

8 How adults support children's mathematical thinking

Guided participation

We have been arguing that young children learn to think mathematically by learning to participate in increasingly knowledgeable ways in the mathematical experiences around them (Saxe *et al.* 1987; Rogoff 1990, 1991). This participation involves them in recognizing the mathematics in an experience and in drawing on the mathematical understandings that they have in order to respond to what they see. For example, when Connor measured his boat in the construction corner he did not hold the tape measure tightly to the end of the boat and did not read the tape measure as 'so many' centimetres. He was beginning to participate mathematically in a construction experience and recognized some aspects of measuring but did not have the mathematical understandings that would allow him to respond in a way that would satisfy, for example, a more expert 10-year-old.

Once one thinks of learning as increasingly knowledgeable responses to the world, the role of adults becomes one of guiding the participation so that a more knowledgeable understanding of the world is constructed by children. It is tempting to think of a curriculum as something we simply pass on to children. But all that we have said about the difficulty of learning number tells us that we need to listen carefully to how young learners are making sense as we assist them to see more and learn how to respond to what they see.

We can best listen and assist in activities that we can share with children. Munn and Schaffer found that good quality interactions in which pre-school professionals seemed to be supporting the learning of 2- to 3-year-olds in literacy and numeracy were far more likely to occur where adults worked with smaller groups of children and used a key worker system (Munn and Schaffer 1993). However, they also noted that interactions based on numeracy were generally infrequent. Most of the numeracy activities they observed occurred as parts of stories or songs and were not found in other shared activities. It seemed as if the adults were not aware of the mathematical potential in, for example, shared games or meal times. Kleinburg and Menmuir (1995) used a wider definition of mathematical activity than Munn and Schaffer and found more widespread evidence of these activities. However, they noted that staff were uncertain about what to categorize as a mathematical event and felt that they needed to improve their own mathematical knowledge.

As we have suggested in Figure 7.2 (see page 123), guiding the increasingly knowledgeable participation of children as mathematical thinkers in pre-school provision seems to require three types of knowledge from early years professionals:

- knowledge of what specific children already understand;
- knowledge of the mathematics that is available in the experiences provided;
- knowledge of how to pace their support for children's learning. We shall look at each of these in turn.

Assessing children's mathematical understanding

Our research partners rapidly concluded that their curriculum development work had to be based on very detailed observations of children as learners. Observational assessment was important for evaluating the experiences they were designing and also for sharing their information on the children as learners with everyone with whom the child would be interacting (see Chapter 3 for further discussion of observations).

Most of the settings kept records of the planned activities that each child experienced. All of them made observational records of children and used them as a basis for their planning for each child. They kept these up to date in a variety of ways. A number of settings used 'post-its' or 'peel off' labels to make immediate notes about what children were understanding in a joint activity and transferred these to the records that were discussed regularly. Others stuck activity record sheets to the walls in areas of the pre-school settings and used them to make notes on the children, which were immediately available to other adults using the area. Another setting listed the understandings they wanted to see in action and colleagues carried a child's list while working with him or her and marked off the behaviours with a highlighter pen as they appeared.

Alison and Melissa used the observation schedules we had developed as part of the research and allocated staff to do regular detailed observations of specific children which were then shared. We know, for example, how Connor tackled measurement because we have Polaroid photographs of him measuring and Alison's notes on the activity made under the following headings:

- Who was involved?
- Why you were observing.
- The general intended purpose of the activity, major resources etc.
- The learning opportunities for these children in the activity.
- What happened.
- What the children seemed to learn (with evidence).
- What the adults learnt.

These headings picked up themes that we have been outlining in this chapter such as 'what these children can get out of this activity' and 'what the children can do and understand'. The headings remind the observer to find a focus – that is, 'which children' and 'what aspect of their learning'. They are also open-ended enough to allow the observer to note unexpected events. We can see the flexibility of the schedule in the following example. Toni (the assistant manager of the centre) is observing Owen who is 36 months.

Who was involved?
Owen aged 3 and Toni, in the construction area, 10.30, 15.5.1998.

Why were you observing?
To assess whether Owen knew the names of shapes (especially rectangle). The staff in blue/green room noted that Owen does not use the construction area. He is quite new to the centre and still finding his feet.

The general intended purpose of the activity
Assess and develop Owen's understanding of shapes (rectangles).

The learning opportunities for these children in the activity
I'm still uncertain what Owen knows. He has still to become familiar with the construction area. Owen will be able to handle and use shapes while I help with names.

What happened
In five minutes during free choice. The full range of equipment was available. Owen was not particularly interested in the construction area before the session. He did not know what a rectangle was. He wanted to go out and play and was embarrassed at being the focus of my attention. He didn't seem to care whether he knew a rectangle or not.

What the children seemed to learn
Owen was not very interested.

What the adults learnt

It was not very successful and it felt odd and artificial. I had tried to coax Owen into an area he wasn't interested in, at a time when he wanted to play outside, to talk about shapes which he was also not interested in. He is still new to the nursery. I needed to go at his pace so I could have used the words for shapes during our conversations outside. Re: the construction area, I could encourage him to build with the crates and boxes outside.

(Later Toni added the following reflection drawn from Wood 1988 to her notes. While children over 5 are 'recruited' to the curriculum you need to 'capture' the imagination and interest of younger children.)

Toni's observation of Owen had been informed by earlier observations made by colleagues and was shared at the next meeting with colleagues so that others were able to follow her advice on interacting with him.

Knowing the mathematics available in an experience

This is a crucial factor in the guidance that adults can give and explains why so much emphasis has been placed on teachers' 'subject knowledge' in primary schools. However, we prefer to talk of 'curriculum knowledge' as that phrase helpfully places some boundaries on what early years workers need to know. We define curriculum knowledge in pre-school settings as the knowledge opportunities that early years workers offer young learners.

The warp and the weft of curriculum knowledge are (i) *content* – what it is we want children to understand and (ii) *orientation* – how we would like children to tackle the experiences we offer them. These two strands are fundamental to every curriculum area. In the area of mathematics the content would include, for example, using cardinal numbers or distinguishing between a square and a rectangle. Orientation would include a disposition to engage with the experience (see Chapter 4), but most specifically a disposition to engage mathematically. That is, to show a way of thinking that will stand the child in good stead when working mathematically when older. Depending on the age of the child, mathematical orientation may include finding a way of remembering where she or he started to count, organizing objects into sets, aiming at accuracy when weighing or measuring, learning to record his or her mathematical thinking, recognizing patterns and so on. In summary, to see the mathematics in situations children need to acquire mathematical habits of mind.

The warp and the weft of curricula become clear as early years professionals plan for children's learning. Team planning helps everyone understand the potential for learning lying in each activity and prepares them for supporting children's developing understandings and orientations.

Melissa and her colleagues in their High Scope pre-school were using the research partnership to both enrich the mathematics experiences provided for their 3- and 4-year-olds and to update their own understandings of the curricular potential in the activities available. Melissa used the observation headings we discussed in the previous section as the basis of her planning meetings. Colleagues identified the children who were to have the experience under discussion and the meetings focused on the reasons for observation, the purposes of the activity and the learning potential in the activity for the children being targeted, so that everyone could understand what mathematics was available in the activity. The remaining sections of the schedule were completed during an observation of a target child.

One of the most important features in Melissa's project turned out to be the impact that team planning had on her colleagues. The impact was seen in two ways: (i) they had a clear focus for their own observations and actions to support children as learners; (ii) their observations and discussions of them made Melissa's colleagues more aware of what the children understood and how they were able to respond when tasks were made slightly more demanding. In summary, armed with greater understanding of the learning potential in activities they were more confident and flexible in the challenge and support they provided for the children.

In Melissa's nursery we observed a group of staff who were becoming increasingly confident in their own capacity to see the mathematics in children's experiences. Research on infant school teachers and the way that they think about mathematics (Aubrey 1997b) shows very clearly how teachers' own understandings and beliefs about the subject shape the way that they organize mathematics in their classrooms and interact with children in mathematics sessions. In our partnership some people were alert to the mathematics in almost every aspect of nursery life to the extent that a striped T-shirt could not be worn without some impromptu pattern game. Others found that they had to plan in fine detail and specify language to be used in order to ensure that mathematics occurred.

However, we would argue that the knowledge base of a fully-fledged early education profession should have an awareness of children's early mathematical understanding as a major strand so that pre-school professionals don't fall into the trap identified by De Corte *et al.* (1996:

508) and limit their teaching to 'a discrete set of goals'. Instead, guided participation means that adults need to be able to work interactively with children so that they follow a child in order to lead. Following in order to lead means that early years workers need to recognize the variety of learning opportunities available in specific experiences and be alert to how they can connect the learning child to the curricular opportunities available. But as Toni found, capturing young children's attention and connecting them to the opportunities for learning isn't easy!

Pacing support for children as learners

In their study of children from 2 years and 6 months to 5, and their mothers, Saxe *et al.* (1987) found that children were learning through being given opportunities to build on number strategies they already possessed in order to deal with new mathematical demands in activities. The mothers achieved this by gradually making the level of joint activities slightly more demanding. They did this by changing the activity, for example, by first playing a card game with low numbers and then including higher number cards in the game, or by gradually withdrawing the help they gave in reading the numbers on the cards so that the child had to count the hearts or spades in order to 'read' the number.

One way of interpreting the mother's role is to see it simply as modelling how to play the game and then raising the task demand just enough for her child to be able to use the skills she or he already had as he or she acquires new ones. But this is to underplay the joint nature of the activity, the frequency with which it was played and its history in the relationship of the mother and her child, its playfulness and the emotional security provided by the mother–child relationship. Guided participation is clearly valuable but needs careful organization if it is to become a central part of the repertoire of early years workers.

Joint activities were central to Melissa's practice. Records of her planning meetings show how she emphasized being a role model and then an observer or listener. The notes from one meeting gives some flavour.

> The role of the adults in the construction area (children are to be encouraged to use play people so that they need to use the language of position – in, on, outside etc.)
>
> 1 Role model: while working with children, adults talk about where the child is putting the play people, vehicles and furniture to stimulate discussion and child talk.

2 Observer/listener: the adult observes and listens to the child's actions and interactions. This will provide knowledge of the child's skills and evidence on which to base further interactions.

Of course one cannot be a role model without being in the action. In the next extract we see Sarah after the planning meeting noted above with two children aged 4 years and 4 months and 4 years and 2 months. They are in the construction area, have just built a tower block of flats like those outside the nursery and are placing play people on the tower.

Sarah: I really think it's like the flats. Is that right?
Child 1:   Mmm, yeh, Look at 'em on top.
Child 2:   Look, four – one, two, three, four.
Sarah: Oh yes. There are four people on top of the flats and they are all looking that way (*points*). Who's at the bottom?
Child 1:   It's a boy. He's going out to play. Look she lives upstairs (*pointing*).
Sarah: Oh I can see. She lives above the boy. What's she called?
Child 2:   Sarah (*giggles*).
Sarah: Same name as me then. That's good.
Child 1:   That one's me (*pointing*).
Sarah: Are you going to the bottom, the top, or are you in the middle?
Child 2:   She's not. She's not.
Sarah: No, not at the top, not at the bottom, not in the middle! But where? Where do you call that?
Child 2:   Nearly. Nearly the top – nearly the middle. If she is up, then top (*moves figure up the tower*).

In this extract we see that Sarah was involved in a playful activity with the two children; was looking at the activity, in part, through their eyes; was able conversationally to extend the activity; and, through the conversation and playfulness (for example, 'where do you call that?'), was able to provide spaces for the children to contribute and construct understandings. Sarah's primary purpose was not to test the children, but a great deal of useful information about the children is revealed and Sarah is able to build on it as the conversation continues. In summary, she was helping the children to see more of the mathematics available in the activity and to find the wherewithal to deal with it. She was assisted in both aims by being part of the action.

In Chapter 4 we talked about how adults can support the learning of young children. Here we see Sarah giving that support – that is, providing help and challenge, for the thinking of two 4-year-olds. We emphasized that giving support is not simply a question of explaining and then leaving the child to work with the activity. Rather, it is more like an interactive dance requiring that the adult assist, stand back and assist again if the child needs it. Pacing the support requires being attuned to the child's way of seeing and responding but also being aware of the overall structure of the dance and the possibilities within it. Pacing also, therefore, needs to take into account children's developmental needs.

In Chapter 4 we discussed how the help adults give can aim at bringing children to understand the world more effectively and that it has slightly different purposes as children develop. In that chapter we talked of the initial intersubjective relationship that carers have with babies, how carers help children to explore the world beyond that relationship and finally how, through sound relationships with the adults in their worlds, children are helped to act increasingly independently.

Our research partners found that the most important feature of their work over the two years of the project was not the activities that they designed to help children to use number. Rather it was the quality of the staff interactions around the activities. In our final workshop, therefore, we identified ways in which adults can support children as learners who are developing a disposition to engage with mathematics. These are shown in Table 8.1.

Table 8.1 Principles of practice in supporting pleasurable participation in mathematics

What we are looking for in children	What adults can do
0–12 months	
• Pleasurable responses	• Give warmth and pleasure
• Alertness	• Model
• Exploration	• Play sorting games
	• Find patterns in songs
Later	• Find consistent patterns in games
• Building	• Find consistent behaviour in routines
• Sorting	• Play body-parts games
• Posting	• Do counting with finger food
• Putting things in	• Sing number rhymes (e.g. 1, 2, 3, 4, 5 etc)
	• Share (e.g. at meal time)
12–18 months	
• Sorting by size and building	• As above
• Posting	• Encourage modelling by older children
• Exploration	and adults

- Joining-in singing
- One-to-one
- Matching with guidance
- Enjoy water and sand

- Water play
- Make the most of domestic situations (e.g. mealtimes)
- Dressmaking
- Dressing
- Gardening
- Cooking
- Sing number songs children can join in
- Allowing children to be part of adults' experience
- Allow children to anticipate patterns in

18–24 months

- Full and empty
- Know number rhymes
- Matching

At 24 months
- Have partners (e.g. walking in twos)
- Imitate language patterns
- Be responsive
- Take initiative with number

- As above, slightly more focused
- Make more demands on child (e.g. get me two pots)
- Give instructions (e.g. walking in twos)
- Sing more rhymes
- Counting stairs/steps
- Allow help with setting table and putting away
- Sorting
- In the park (e.g. see-saw, up-down)
- Thinking aloud when using numbers

24–36 months

- Purposeful/systematic behaviour
- Concrete use of, e.g., 2
- Start of understanding of quality
- Using mathematical language

- As above, slightly more focused
- Children asked to set table
- Help children with matching games
- Ask children questions which require numerical answers
- Help children make collections (e.g. buttons, shells)

36–60 months

- Closer relationship between language and accepted meaning
- Appear to be getting more from working with other children
- Ordinal/cardinal differences
- Start sensible estimates
- Start symbolic recording (iconic)
- Number as *fun*

- As above, more focused, higher expectations of children's language use
- Play guessing games using number
- Help with sorting collections into sets
- Model measuring, recording etc.
- Provide materials to extend children's mathematical thinking
- Play number games

Providing mathematical experiences

In Chapter 4 we explained that learning involves becoming competent at using the tools of a culture. These tools include the language of mathematics (how we count or name shapes and the language formats of mathematics such as 'one more'), ways of working in mathematics (how we record our mathematical thinking or emphasize accuracy) and material artefacts (a tape measure or a weighing scale). In the present chapter we have discussed how children experience mathematical activities at their level of competence and have shown that part of the role of adults is to help them extend that competence by seeing other opportunities in the activity. Therefore, although we shall now discuss a number of the curricular opportunities that were developed in the partnership we stress that children will work with them in a variety of ways and adult support should tailor the activity to the strengths and needs of children.

We know that children enter formal schooling at 5 with a considerable amount of mathematical cultural capital. That is, they have had experience of, for example, number, shape and capacity, and use what they have gained from these experiences as the foundation of their mathematical learning in school. However, children's capital can vary quite considerably due to differences between their environments in the first five years of life (Aubrey *et al.* 2003). One of the purposes of pre-school educational provision is to ensure that as many children as possible experience the activities that provide valuable capital. We have been arguing that pre-school provision is therefore not meant to be a watered down version of school but a pedagogically enriched version of the worlds they inhabit.

Our research partners operated with that principle very much in mind as they developed materials and activities in their settings. A strong feature in almost all the activities developed was their 'every-dayness'. These were, for example, activities that would be found in the homes of most advantaged children made slightly more focused by the careful resourcing and sensitive interventions of staff. We shall look at some of the activities and research projects by grouping them rather arbitrarily under three headings: birth to 18 months, 18 months to 3 years and 3 to 5 years. These phases broadly represent the phases from intersubjectivity to independence that we outlined in Chapter 4.

Birth to 18 months

A songbook

Millie and Amy's centre is situated on an estate near a city centre and is used by parents who work in the city as well as by local residents. Babies are taken when they are 3 months old and stay in the baby room until they are toddlers and need more space. Millie and Amy were keen to provide continuity of care with the children's homes and produced the songbook we mentioned in Chapter 4 when we discussed intersubjectivity. The songs in the book were selected to augment the children's mathematical capital. There were number rhymes (e.g. 'Round and round the garden'); songs with repetitive patterns (e.g. 'Pat-a-cake' and 'Peep-o'); and songs associated with bath time or dressing and parts of the body (e.g. 'Two little eyes').

The songbooks were welcomed both by the young mothers who lived locally and the busy working mothers, and alerted them to how they could playfully help their children to become receptive to number. Millie and Amy involved all the staff in compiling the book and simultaneously alerted them to the value of number songs as a fun way of bringing number into the experiences they offered children throughout the nursery.

Building on experiences from several cultures

Reza, a multicultural services officer, and June, the head of an inner-city pre-school, decided to explore the capital that the children were bringing to the nursery from their homes. Children in the pre-school between them spoke 20 languages. June and Reza invited parents to a meeting to discuss their project and emphasized how keen they were to ensure that the pre-school was aware of what the children were learning at home.

June visited five of the families regularly and listened as the parents chatted about their children's growing interest in the mathematics around them. An important learning point for June and her colleagues was that the parents used songs in very different ways from that suggested by the pre-school. Songs were sung by the whole family in Arabic-speaking homes and were sung for different purposes – for example, ballads for storying, lullabies at bedtime and strongly rhythmical songs for dancing.

Importantly, the learning was two-way. The parents became more aware of how they could help their children see the numbers around them as they grew older and the pre-school staff learnt that they needed to work with the cultural opportunities available in the children's homes and develop materials that fitted into the rhythms and richness of the children's cultural lives at home. Parents were invited to contribute their own family favourites to a multilingual nursery songbook.

18 months to 3 years

A musical curriculum

Frances runs a workplace centre which takes children from 2 years of age. Songs and singing lie at the core of Frances's practice. As part of their project Frances and her colleagues brainstormed the *skills*, *concepts* and *attitudes* involved in making music. They came up with the following list:

Listening	concentrating	discriminating
organizing	cooperation	fine and gross motor control
consideration	discussion	memory
self-discipline	problem solving	sharing
decision-making	independence	imagination
critical awareness	mutual respect	tolerance
perseverance	sense of achievement	caring
enthusiasm	positive self-image	confidence
enjoyment	curiosity	empathy

As the project progressed they saw that they could combine these important curricular aims with focuses which gave children mathematical experiences. These included clapping to musical patterns, sitting in large and small circles, ordering children by size in action songs, number rhymes involving counting, some simple rhymes involving making sets of children or objects and using cardinal numbers, adding or removing one child or object at a time, and action games requiring children to work in pairs and match actions. Songs such as 'Peter hammers with one hammer' played an important part in the children's introduction to number as fun.

In all of these examples the familiar patterns of the songs acted as a form of scaffolding in which younger children could first see adults and other children model behaviour, and then imitate the actions and appropriate the language before being able to fully understand the rules and meanings of the activity.

Making the most of everyday mathematics

Josie runs a large pre-school school on the outskirts of a city. Everywhere you turn in the setting you see evidence of children's mathematical thinking. Colour mixing activities lead to pattern making, the progress of the newly-hatched ducklings is monitored using counting, short sorting activities or number games greet parents and children as they arrive at the school, one-to-one matching occurs in the home, construction, design and technology areas and recording is built into role-play in the shop or cafe. Josie and her colleagues clearly have mathematical thinking as a priority. Josie was keen that parents shared her enthusiasm for mathematics, not only to help the children already attending the pre-school, but also to prepare younger family members. Preparation is important, as local school placement policies mean that children stay in Josie's setting for no longer than a year. Children therefore need to be ready to make the most of the opportunities available to them when they arrive.

Josie was already familiar with the excellent work on parental involvement in primary school mathematics carried out by the IMPACT project team (Merttens and Vass 1990, 1993) and wanted to build on their ideas as she strengthened relationships with her parents. She started by inviting parents of children entering the pre-school to a 30-minute meeting where she talked about the mathematical learning children are experiencing at home. Parents' interest in the topic led to a series of evening meetings and a partnership with the local adult education services which set up afternoon classes for interested parents on 'parents as partners' in their children's education. The major themes in Josie's work with parents were acknowledging what parents had to offer and encouraging them to see just how mathematically rich the home environment is.

After exploring the learning opportunities at home with their own young children the parents made booklets for other parents on, for example, maths in the bathroom, maths at mealtimes, maths in the kitchen. Parents also took pictures of their children sorting shoes into pairs, making sets of lipsticks and nail varnishes, counting steps in the garden and so on. The photographs were then shared and discussed at parents' meetings. We met the parents who were involved several times during the project and found their enthusiasm and inventiveness inexhaustible and their appreciation of what the nursery school was doing with their children while they were there impressive.

Working with childminders to make the most of everyday mathematics

Gill was the only childminder involved in the project. She set up regular meetings of a small group of childminders and discussed the ideas that were being discussed in the project. Gill reported that they focused on 'spontaneously available learning opportunities' which occurred from 'children's everyday activities or interests'. At meetings the group brainstormed ideas about everyday mathematical experiences such as seeing shapes, playing with patterns and using number.

They all kept a daily numeracy diary in which they logged activities which could offer the children opportunities for mathematical thinking. At their meetings they discussed what they did to enhance children's mathematical experiences. Areas of activity focused on patterns and shape; comparisons and problem solving in, for example, cooking or planning a day out; the language of position, size and shape in, for example, games and putting things away; and numbers in the world about them, in counting games and in dressing.

They felt strongly that they needed to be alert to the opportunities in activities and enjoyed being able to evaluate their own roles in encouraging children to participate in those opportunities. In summary, they had the advantage of strong and consistent links with the children they saw (usually daily) and were also able to think as practitioners about how to assist children as learners.

3 to 5 years

We have already discussed at some length the mathematical experiences provided by Alison and Melissa in their construction areas. In our discussions we emphasized three features:

- careful resourcing – for example, the tape measure and recording opportunities in Alison's project and the play people in Melissa's;
- the open-ended nature of the opportunities they provided so that children could work with the skills they had;
- the playfully interactive role of the adults so that they could model language and responses and raise the demands of the activity when necessary.

Other examples from our partnership included Bernie's project with Claire, the teacher in an inner-city multicultural pre-school and Jade's work in the outer-city centre where she was the teacher attached to the pre-school.

Number as an international language

Bernie, like Reza, worked for the city's multicultural services and was attached to Claire's pre-school. Together, they decided to focus on specific cardinal numbers and give children the opportunity to work with a variety of sets of one cardinal number over the period of one month at a time. They decided to focus on the target numeral to enhance children's number literacy, regardless of their ability to speak English. The one-month focus on each number allowed parental involvement by providing sets of small objects (e.g. coins or buttons) and number songs from home, and gave time to work with the numbers in the children's mother tongues as well as in English. The tight focus and long timescale also helped to secure the attention of volunteer workers to the pre-school's curricular aims.

Activities in the 'fives' month included: number rhymes such as 'Five in a bed' and 'Five little speckled frogs' with song cards to take home; the collection of sets of fives for display; organizing children into groups of five for activities; sorting objects into sets of five; finding ways of recording five; writing fives in the sand; setting the table in the home area for five people; planting five seedlings in pots; feely bags with five objects in them; clapping rhythms with five beats; building the longest road with five blocks, and so on.

Everyday mathematics in the neighbourhood

Jade's project was beset by problems including vandalism and flooding. However, she did not give up. Parental involvement was a priority for the centre in which she was the pre-school teacher. The centre is situated on an estate on the edge of a large city, not far from a large out-of-town shopping mall. The parents are mainly young single parents who have strong negative feelings about school based on their own quite recent experiences as pupils. There is also a small Urdu-speaking population. Parents see the centre primarily as a place for care and not for education.

To encourage parental confidence in the centre's abilities to help their children value learning, Jade planned a mathematics trail in the shopping mall. She used the trail to highlight the everyday mathematical experiences that children and parents might share on a visit to the shops. She and her colleagues produced two information packs. One focused on shapes and used photographs that staff had taken at the mall. The photographs included shop signs, patterns of windows, floor tiles, fabric patterns and a map of the mall. The second pack consisted of a set of questions or prompts to guide parents' conversations as they walked around the mall with their children. The questions or prompts included:

'Look at the floors, walls and ceiling. What patterns can you see?'; 'Can you see any triangles?'; 'What numbers can you see in the shop windows?'

The first pack was discussed with parents at a meeting before the visit to the mall. Parents were then given the second pack as they set off for the mall with their children and some of the centre staff. While they were on the trail, staff modelled how to help the children see the everyday mathematics around them and encouraged the parents to do the same. Parents took photographs of their children having fun with mathematics.

The photographs were enjoyed at a follow-up meeting with the parents arranged by Jade. At the meeting there were more conversations about the mathematics that were experienced and parents' confidence in their abilities to help their children use aspects of mathematics was again encouraged. A book about shape and number based on the visit was produced in both English and Urdu and was made available to all parents.

Summary

Our research partnership consisted of a network of people who aimed at trialing a small number of activities in either numeracy or literacy for children from birth to 5. Consequently we are not offering an exhaustive list of tips for early years workers. Even if that had been our intention we would have been deterred by the feedback we received from our research partners. The messages from the pre-school settings was that far more important than the activities provided is the quality of the interaction that occurs around them. We therefore are not offering the activities mentioned in this chapter as blueprints for a pre-school mathematics curriculum. Instead we are suggesting a careful process of trial and evaluation that emphasizes attention to both what the children and the staff are learning as they engage with the mathematical opportunities available in pre-school settings and at home.

Suggested reading

A detailed and useful introduction to the theory and the practice of providing mathematical experiences in pre-schools is Montague-Smith, A. (1997) *Mathematics in Nursery Education* (London: David Fulton).

Leone Burton, a well-known writer in the area of mathematics education, has looked at young children's mathematical narratives in a paper that reminds us of children's capabilities as they make sense and discuss their sense-making in mathematics. Burton, L. (2002) Children's mathematical narratives as learning stories, *European Early Childhood Education Research Journal,* 10 (2): 5–18.

If you are interested in teachers' knowledge and its impact on how mathematics is taught in the early years, Carol Aubrey's account of the thinking and practice of infant teachers is a comprehensive study of this topic: Aubrey, C. (1997a) *Mathematics Teaching in the Early Years* (London: Falmer).

9 Creating contexts for professional development

Times of change

As we outlined in Chapter 1 the project took place during a time of rapid change affecting early childhood services in the UK and, as we saw in Chapter 2, in the years that followed the pace of change continued. An important feature of more recent policy, in the UK and elsewhere, has been to expect practitioners to work collaboratively across professional boundaries and to encourage them to work with the family networks which support children as well as with the children themselves. These expectations are leading to new forms of practice which have at their core the well-being and social inclusion of children. Elsewhere we have suggested that these new forms of practice include the following features (Edwards 2004a):

- a focus on children and as whole people i.e. not as specific 'needs';
- following the child's trajectory overtime and across services;
- an ability to talk across professional boundaries;
- an understanding of what other practitioners are able to offer the responsive package of protection or care that is built around the child or young person;
- acknowledgement of the capacity of service users and their families to help to tailor the services they are receiving;
- an understanding that changing the life trajectories of children involves not only building confidence and skills but also a reconfiguring of the opportunities available to them through systems-wide change.

In many ways our project, as we said in Chapter 3, created a boundary zone where people could operate outside their own workplaces, learn to talk across organizational boundaries and make their own expertise explicit in conversations about evidence. There was also, as we have seen, an emphasis on working with parents and drawing them into learning partnerships with practitioners. However, expectations for inter-professional collaboration and working with families and communities are even higher now.

In this chapter we look at professional learning in a changing system: the learning of individuals; the contexts in which their learning takes place; and what this learning means for practice, training and management. We use the term 'learning' rather than 'coping' not simply because we want to avoid the rather negative tone of coping, but also because we believe that dealing with change is a matter of simply learning something new and taking a positive approach to that learning. Even better is when they can communicate this excitement about learning to the children's parents or main carers. We are therefore optimistic that an area of provision that has expertise in helping children learn will also be good at helping adults learn.

All that we have discussed in the last five chapters tells us that sound quality interactions with adults are central to the development of children's dispositions to learn. It is a truism, but nonetheless a powerful one, that children learn to love learning through being with adults who also love to learn, and are themselves in contexts that encourage their learning. This truism, therefore, means that children deserve to be supported by adults who are driven by their own intellectual curiosity to understand their practice better. Children's learning, we would argue, is supported by a system that has the learning of both children and adults as a priority.

Supporting the learning of practitioners

In Chapter 4 we outlined features of learning in early childhood. A number of these features also apply to how pre-school workers learn and how they can be supported. In our project the learning goals for practitioners, like those for the children, focused on the *who* as much as on the *what* of learning and particularly on helping participants develop a capacity to interpret and respond to the learning opportunities available for children. The goals included:

- developing the capacity to see the educational potential in experiences shared with children;
- developing the capacity to respond to the demands they have identified as they work with children;
- developing dispositions for enquiry and learning;
- developing ways of seeing and being which draw on the professional expertise of early years practitioners.

Like children, adults learn best in safe and well-supported contexts where they are able to learn through a form of *guided participation* (Rogoff 1991). Guided participation is important because we are suggesting that enhancing professional practice is a question of learning to interpret familiar events in fresh ways and developing a repertoire of responses to new interpretations. Fresh interpretations and responses usually need to be modelled or guided and can seem quite risky. Interpretations might be wrong and responses may misfire. Practitioners need support if they are to persevere in changing their practices.

Support for practitioners' learning through guided participation occurred in two ways in the project (see Chapter 3 for an outline of the project as three steps):

1. collaboration between higher education, local authority officers and the key participants in Steps 1 and 2;
2. collaboration within settings on action research in Step 3.

During these *collaborations* practitioners' learning was supported by:

- the modelling of strategies with children by more expert practitioners – for example, when Mollie worked with children on mark-making and was observed by a colleague;
- discussions for planning and reviewing;
- joint data collection and analysis;
- shared frameworks for data collection – for example, observation schedules;
- a shared focus on children's learning in numeracy and literacy.

Practitioners' learning became evident in how they used language (for example, the idea of joint involvement episodes became central to several projects); and in how the familiar materials of pre-school provision took on new educational meanings. For example, the construction area became a site for children's early mark-making in one setting and their mathematical thinking and action in another.

In the structured and non-threatening learning contexts provided by the project, practitioners were able, in their discussions, to *appropriate* the frameworks and language of early learning shared in the workshops and readings. Similarly, while they worked with these new ideas with children they were able to identify the educational potential of familiar materials – such as how blocks and play people could be used together to develop children's use of mathematical language in a fantasy play context – and respond knowledgeably.

We were interested to note in our repertory grid analysis discussed in

Chapter 3 (see Table 3.3) that participants did not identify a need for new resources as a result of an increased emphasis on curricula. Instead, and our field notes would confirm this, existing materials were being given new (educational) meanings by practitioners. The changes appeared to be in the way the adults were interpreting events and responding while working with children. The professional learning that occurred through well-supported participation in new forms of practice seemed considerable. The adults learnt through developing new ideas, representations, or ways of thinking about familiar occurrences in project meetings. They then took these ideas into action in their action research projects. But like children, adults can only change their ways of thinking and acting in contexts that allow these changes to occur. Learning contexts for adults, therefore, need careful management.

Current work on educational settings as learning organizations

Our emphasis on the *who* of learning – that is, the development of informed professional identities capable of making the responsive decisions that are so much part of supporting young children as learners – led us to examine the strategies that the most successful managers used to support the professional development of colleagues.

There is a vast literature on school development, some of which focuses on educational change through the professional development of teachers. So much valuable work has been undertaken in this field that it would be somewhat narrow-minded of early education professionals if they were to ignore it. The work we shall discuss has been influenced by methods of person-centred organizational development found in commercial and industrial organizations. The approach emphasizes professional learning as the key to informed responses to external changes. Michael Fullan's (1991) comprehensive review of research on educational change in the contexts of educational reform in North America provides many useful pointers for institution-based professional learning for early years professionals. Above all he reminds us that changing hearts and minds is also a question of changing cultures, that change is usually complex and rarely straightforward, that it needs to be managed by supporting the learning of colleagues as they develop new ideas in practice, that it takes time and is far more than a question of simply setting targets.

We outlined our project as a change process in Chapter 3. The goal of our project was not simply to ensure that our practitioner partners could deliver *Desirable Outcomes for Learning* (DfEE/SCAA 1996). We could not even assume that the document would still be in use at the end of the project, given recent policy swings. Instead we wanted to ensure that they were able to develop strategies for dealing with changing contexts in informed ways. We intended that the project would give key participants experiences of frameworks for evidence-based practice which would help them develop their colleagues as practitioners. Our focus was therefore as much on the adults as learners as on the pupils. We were therefore also interested, as outsiders at least, in the settings as learning communities.

Louis *et al.* (1996), in a detailed study of teachers' professional communities identified five components which they found to be significant in schools as learning communities which in turn supported children as learners. These components were:

1. a shared sense of purpose;
2. a collective focus on pupil learning;
3. collaborative activity;
4. deprivatized activity;
5. reflective dialogues.

A shared sense of purpose takes time to achieve and cannot be imposed. Quite often a sense of coherent purpose only emerges in the processes of discussion and action as colleagues clarify exactly what they mean by, for example, the community values underpinning the work of a preschool centre. Fullan (1991, 1993) points out that one sign that change is not really happening is when people demonstrate 'false clarity' – for example, the rhetoric is spoken and accepted but the implications for practice are barely explored. Parental involvement is an area where false clarity is frequently seen. False clarity is evident, for example, when parental involvement is discussed as a 'good thing' without anyone being clear about what they really think parents can do to help their children learn. In our study, as we shall see later in this chapter, our colleagues took the time necessary to move way beyond any sense of false clarity in their work with parents and identified coherent rationales for parental involvement.

A collective focus on pupil learning allows the development of a professional discourse which centres on the professional actions of colleagues as they create contexts and plan and evaluate actions taken to support children's learning. In our study two strong themes in the collective focus on children's learning were (i) detailed and clearly focused observations of how children were making sense of the opportunities available to them and (ii) careful consideration of how adults interacted with children while they engaged with the materials provided.

Collaborative activity is essential for the development of a professional discourse of multi-agency practice and the professional learning of practitioners. We have proposed that learning occurs as people take action and interpret and react to events in increasingly informed ways – i.e. as they become people who see and act differently. Knowledge, we have therefore argued, is constructed in action as well as in discussions of action. Collaborative activity was central to our study, particularly at Step 3 where new understandings developed in Steps 1 and 2 were refined in action in pre-school settings. Here our research partners, having undertaken some small-scale work themselves at Step 2, were able to guide the participation of other colleagues in the practices they were developing.

Deprivatized activity links closely to both a collective focus on learning and taking action together. Compared with schools, most pre-school settings are well placed for ensuring that adults' activities are visible. What did have to be worked at was finding space for the open discussion of activities in which new practices were tried out or modelled. Key activities became the focus of frequent staff meetings in which areas for action were identified, strategies selected and the evidence gathered during the activities was discussed. Early childhood services in Reggio Emilia similarly emphasize deprivatized activity in the stress they place on documenting their work to ensure that their practices are visible to colleagues and parents (Edwards *et al.* 1993). These documents not only render expert practice visible but enable colleagues to respond more coherently to children.

Reflective dialogues, in which evidence either about the settings or action taken is discussed, encourage careful observation and analysis and the sharing of insights and information. But above all they ensure that the tacit expertise of professionals is revealed. Reflective dialogues were a feature of all three steps in our project and occurred between higher education and the key settings-based participants at Step 1, between higher education, key participants and their colleagues at Step 2 and mainly between the key participants and their immediate colleagues at Step 3. These conversations were the vehicles for knowledge exchange and joint knowledge construction and were carefully built into project planning in every step.

We did not explore the supervision systems at work in the collaborating settings in this project. However, there is evidence to suggest that supervisory practices which focus on professional issues, attend to the personal development of practitioners, emphasize the learning of individuals and groups and allow roles and practices to develop responsively are found in cultures usually described as developmental or learning (Hawkins and Shohet 1989). We would argue that supervisory systems for early education practitioners in many ways parallel key worker systems for children. Good quality supervision which focuses on how adults are helping children develop as learners and encourages reflective dialogue based on evidence and joint activities may prove to be one important driver of change in early years provision.

Working for professional development across institutional boundaries

We have so far outlined two levels of change in the development of pre-school professional practice: (i) individual professional learning and (ii) institutional strategies to support professional learning. As our focus in this chapter is the professional development of early years practitioners we now turn to examine how professional learning in our research project was enhanced through working across professional and locational boundaries and through opening up practice to ideas that refreshed and, at times, transformed it.

Work at the boundaries of institutional settings was an important feature of the project, whether this was with parents, other professional groups, or colleagues in other settings or other local authorities. We would argue that if pre-school practice is to develop as an informed profession able to meet the shifts and challenges of recent policy, informed flexibility is essential. We could see the development of that confident flexibility and responsiveness in the practitioners who worked with us and have subsequently reflected on the features of the project that seem to have enabled it. These reflections have, of course, been informed by other work we have undertaken on multi-agency working (Anning, Cottrell *et al.* 2005; Edwards 2004b; NECF 2004).

As we have already suggested, the project itself seemed to operate as what Konkola (2001) describes as a boundary zone. These zones sit between systems – such as the pre-school settings in our project. They can be described as sites that are free from pre-arranged routines or rigid patterns, where the norms of each of the contributing systems are reflected. People bring their histories to them, but they are multi-voiced spaces and acknowledge the different contexts that are reflected in them. Most importantly though, they work well as sites for learning when they work on a common focus or task. In the project we are describing, the task was how to enhance professional learning to promote children's learning. We have learnt from our other projects that what happens in these sites is that ideas become clarified as people discuss matters of practice and make their expertise explicit. However, they are not sites of practice. They need to be augmented by opportunities to take new ways of thinking into practice. This is where, of course, the action research projects were so effective – though a word of caution is necessary here. The projects were effective in settings where the managers were in agreement with the aims of the wider project. In one setting they were not, and the practitioner had to work outside the system of the setting, with parents, in order to take forward the ideas she had developed in the project (see Edwards 2004b for a more detailed discussion).

In summary, however, the research project itself seemed to become a safe yet challenging space in which meanings could be shared and developed. For example, the project enabled colleagues to operate across the boundaries of their own professional settings and the histories of their own professional backgrounds and to use common research strategies on a set of similar problems associated with children's early learning in literacy and mathematics. As we saw in Chapter 3, practitioners developed the confidence to make their tacitly held professional knowledge explicit in ways that could be shared with other participants and then take them into practice.

We also found other forms of boundary work between projects and their local communities going on around the artefacts that were being developed in the projects. These artefacts were what Star has described as 'boundary objects' (Star 1989). For example, we observed that those projects that involved working with parents passed materials, such as a songbook, between home and school and used these shared materials as opportunities jointly to build understandings of the children as learners both at home and at nursery. These materials included booklets about the children and what they could do, songs and nursery rhymes written on cards or in booklets, and number sets that children had constructed at home. Importantly, these artefacts were used both to enable practitioners to learn about the children as learners at home and to help parents to understand how they could support their children as participants in, for example, literacy while at home.

Boundary zones and also shared artefacts seemed to enable learning across boundaries. Let us therefore look in a little more detail at how learning relationships were sustained through links between settings, other agencies, the community, adult education, higher education, parents, and other types of pre-school provision.

Working with other agencies

Speech therapy

Ivy's project, discussed in Chapter 6, involved her learning while working alongside speech therapists while Ivy herself guided the learning of the mothers on whom her project was focused. Ivy collaborated with speech therapists in devising a tightly focused learning programme for the mothers which aimed at developing their interaction skills with their children. The project drew on the ideas about child development and the importance of good quality relationships with caregivers we have outlined in Chapter 4, and shared in workshops in Steps 1 and 2 of the project. The speech therapists' specialist expertise, their experience in developing communication skills and their familiarity with the nursery were invaluable in both planning and carrying out the programme. The sessions with mothers operated as boundary zones where Ivy, therapists and mothers all focused in children and interactions with them, then mothers took those ideas back into their practices at home.

A local multicultural service

Bernie and Reza work for the multicultural services section of one of the collaborating local authorities. They were also project members who collaborated with teachers in two inner-city nurseries. Bernie's collaboration focused on number use. Working with a group of practitioners in one nursery, he was able to advise practitioners on how to make the most of the cultural strengths that the children, from up to 11 different ethnic backgrounds, brought to the nursery.

For Reza, the project allowed him to explore a long-held professional hunch: that children's musical experiences at home vary across ethnic groups and that this may have an impact on how they are able to engage with number-related learning experiences in nurseries. As we outlined in Chapter 8, he collaborated with June, a nursery-based practitioner, and learnt through the interviews undertaken with parents at home about what the parents from a range of ethnic groupings thought about children's early number experiences at home and in the nursery, and how music was used within each home. Ideas from the home were brought into the school.

An initiative in another city

Jenny's project, discussed in Chapter 6, was part of a wider local authority initiative which aimed at improving literacy. It targeted specific parents of young infants and built on the Bookstart Project in Birmingham (Book Trust 1998). The project had three aims:

1. to encourage parents to share books with their babies;
2. to raise awareness of how literacy develops in very young children;

3. to raise awareness of the parent's role in helping their children to value literacy.

Jenny's evaluations suggest that, although she was working with ideas gathered during an initial visit to the programme in Birmingham from practitioners there, without the locally based support for developing her thinking about present practice that was provided by our project she was in danger of being isolated. The lesson here seems to be that being open to ideas from elsewhere is essential, but taking these ideas into practice in ways that transform practice is helped by locally-based opportunities for frequent and detailed discussion of practice.

Working with parents

Singing from the same song sheet

We discussed the songbook produced by Millie and Amy in Chapter 4. We drew on it as an example of how a nursery tried to provide babies with some consistency of experience when they were enjoying finger rhymes and songs at home and in the nursery. We particularly noticed the use of line drawings which reminded both parents and practitioners of how a baby was most usefully held for a particular rhyme or action song. We highlighted this in discussions with Millie and Amy and in workshops, in relation to two features. First, how consistent action and language formats help children develop as language users, and second how interactive songs help children to engage in the conversational give and take they need to experience as early communicators.

The songbook became a boundary object or shared tool for promoting learning between parents and practitioners when it was being compiled and when it was used. Parents and staff provided songs and when the book was in use they discussed the children's reactions to individual songs. Discussions about the children and songs helped staff to build on children's experiences with their parents. The book also created a space for discussions about informed practice between nursery and university-based practitioners.

Partnership in early literacy

Meg and her staff at her children's centre on a large outer-city council estate had, for a long time, been keen to involve parents in supporting their children as learners. As we outlined in Chapter 6, Meg started with an unstructured book loan scheme for the 3- and 4-year-olds which brought the parents into the centre to choose books with their children. Our advice was that Meg should work with the parents' strengths – i.e. the strong emotional links they have with their children and make sure that anything they asked parents to do was easily managed and was fun. We discussed nursery rhyme cards that we had seen in use in another project and Meg took up the idea.

Meg produced simple cards with rhymes on one side and suggestions on the reverse. These suggestions included actions to accompany the rhyme, help with finding familiar words in the rhyme, help on how to point to print and ideas for using the same sounds to make up your own rhymes. Parents shared their children's enjoyment with staff when they exchanged cards and appeared to have lost their earlier diffidence about how they might support their children as learners. It seemed that the book and card loan scheme with their realistic expectations broke a barrier between home and nursery that had been troubling Meg.

Involving parents and adult learning support services

Josie's project on parental involvement in early mathematical thinking is discussed in Chapter 8. Josie's nursery is situated in an area of private housing on the outskirts of a city. The parents are keen supporters of the nursery and attend in large numbers any workshop or meeting she holds. So keen were the parents during the project that Josie could have found herself becoming an adult educator rather than a pre-school specialist.

The solution was to involve the local authority's adult learning support service. At various stages in the project this service provided regular classes for parents which had the effect of raising parents' own sense of self-efficacy and leading them to either job-seeking or further training. The service also provided workshops in the pre-school on early number development at home.

We would suggest that involving adult education services is an option that is always worth exploring as local targets for women's access to training or the participation of certain ethnic groups in local training opportunities may mean that funding is easily available. Josie certainly valued the support provided. She brought the adult educator quite centrally into the project, and developed ideas with her.

These brief outlines of several of the individual projects illustrate four key features found in each of them:

1. a coherent sense of purpose;
2. a strong sense of the possible;

3. an openness to new possibilities;
4. an openness to new relationships.

We would suggest that these features are essential in pre-school settings in order for them to deal with the rapidly changing contexts in which they are operating.

The project as a learning network

We designed the project with relationships very firmly in mind. New ways of thinking and acting could not be developed unless relationships across boundaries were possible and new forms of practical knowledge could be generated in joint action. We were influenced in our thinking by the idea of learning networks. We thought that networks would allow participants to bring together the best of current practice, refreshed by external insights, and develop understandings that would allow them to make informed decisions about future practice. In this section we therefore reflect how we operated as a network for learning.

We were aware that our roles as higher education-based researchers in the action research of settings-based practitioners, and in the project as a network, needed exploring. Elliott's (1994) work on teachers' knowledge and action research reminds us of the place of theory and the role of higher education in action research networks. He argues that the ideas of theorists don't threaten practitioners if these ideas can be translated into concrete curriculum proposals that can be scrutinized in action by practitioners who then decide what should be ultimately absorbed into practice. Action research, he suggests, gives the university-based 'theorist' a role as supplier of theoretical resources for practitioners to draw on when analysing and developing practice. However, he emphasizes that the practitioner is the ultimate judge of what is useful knowledge. Elliott's ideas resonate with those of Paul Hirst, who argues that practical reasoning is developed when practice is illuminated by reference to theoretical reasoning (Hirst 1996), and this illumination occurs in conversations about practice.

Elliott's summary of the role of university-based staff in teachers' action research projects is a useful starting point. However, our project as a network did more than simply focus on how individual practitioners developed practical reasoning. Our role involved us in working at three organizational levels: the local authority, the pre-school setting and groups of practitioners. Key stakeholders in each of these levels were crucial to the success of the project and we could not have found ourselves with better collaborators. Each level in turn enabled the next.

The senior local authority officers with whom we planned the project shared our vision and identified experienced and responsible stakeholders at the level of the settings and then did all they could to support the activities at settings level. The experienced settings-based staff became our research partners and, in turn, enabled the responsive activities of their colleagues as they worked with new strategies with children and with other agencies or parents.

This strong, multi-level commitment to the project then served as a sound basis for the learning network we established. Learning a new form of professional practice in the acts of practice can be highly challenging. Work on teacher training, for example, suggests that student teachers are strongly resistant to developing new ways of interpreting classroom events and responding to them (Desforges 1995; Edwards 1998). Part of the difficulty lies in the need for them to experience a destabilization of current understandings before new ones are recognized as necessary. The destabilizing can be professionally threatening when working publicly with children.

Going slowly was therefore essential. At Step 1 we gained agreement on (i) the purposes of the project and (ii) that we would work slowly from evidence gathered in the settings. During Step 1 we spent time at workshops, building relationships through sharing current understandings and concerns, and everyone visited each others' settings. We cannot overestimate the importance of the time taken to establish sound relationships across the network. At two residential meetings and workshops at Steps 2 and 3, participants provided each other with both enthusiastic interest in progress and informed support at times of glitch. Mutual support was an extremely important feature and gives us some confidence in the sustainability of the network we helped to establish.

As we mentioned in Chapter 3, our roles changed over the duration of the project as the practitioners gained control of the presentation of knowledge in discussions and written texts. We were working with our own version of what Huberman (1995) describes as an *open collective cycle* for the generation of changes in the practices of teaching. Huberman's notion of a networked learning cycle is based on the idea of collaboration between several schools that share a common pedagogic focus for their activities. Huberman's cycle is managed by the group of schools that calls in external specialists when required. These external specialists may be from higher education or they may be other specialists. Their roles include what he terms 'conceptual inputs', 'experience sharing', 'help with observations of practice' and the 'analysis of observations'.

Our conceptual inputs were most overt in Step 1 when we ran the topic-based workshops and produced the research summaries we outlined in Chapter 3, and they continued in discussions about practice in Steps 2 and 3. However, conceptual framings were increasingly represented in the contexts of practice by our research partners who appropriated the frameworks we shared and used them in discussions of practice. Experience sharing occurred regularly in workshops and, as we visited each setting, we carried information about developments from one setting to another and shared experiences and practical ideas we had gained elsewhere in similar projects. Help with observations came through advice on observational methods for both exploring practice (see Chapter 3) and formatively assessing children (see Chapter 8). Analysis of observations also occurred during our visits and in workshops. By Step 3, most settings were managing their own evaluations of their work in their own settings.

We saw the network as a set of overlapping communities of understanding, all with the interests of children as learners as a central concern. As researchers we belonged primarily to the research community. Our research partners were primarily practitioners, who themselves belonged to the communities of, for example, either care or education. The senior managers were led by the concerns of that role. We all brought a range of strengths and experiences to the project. We learnt from each other as we moved in and out of the overlapping communities, gathering information and sharing insights drawn from our particular expertise.

What did we two researchers learn? We started the project with a strong belief in the shared wisdom of the people with whom we were working. We learnt very quickly not to underestimate their thirst for information and the capacity to take that information into practice for professional scrutiny. Most importantly, our view that the developments we observed were more about the informed and responsive professionals than about the creation of a curriculum, was substantiated every time we spoke to any of our research partners.

But was a community of practice established through the project? Responses to the questionnaire we discussed in Chapter 3 suggest that only one of the key practitioners thought so. However, the rest were unanimous in thinking that we had, between us, established a community of understanding which would serve to underpin future developments in professional thinking and practice. Given our emphasis on professional practice as informed responsive decision-making we were considerably heartened by these responses.

Contexts for the development of new forms of practice

An informed professional can only work responsively in a context that allows this to happen. This does not mean that professionals are victims of the systems in which they find themselves operating. Neither does it mean that an individual in isolation can change a system and what is allowed to occur within it. Early years practitioners, working together, need to see the possibilities for informed responsive action that are available to them in their settings, and use those possibilities. They need to talk about what they are doing and why they are doing it and so take responsibility for the generation of their own knowledge base.

The development of practice will depend upon the continuous development, in action, of a common store of practical knowledge that is itself constantly open to scrutiny. Such scrutiny can only occur in a professional climate that encourages the confidence to value openness and collaboration across boundaries of profession and location so that the best interests of children are served.

Suggested reading

Rodd, J. (1994) *Leadership in Early Childhood* (Buckingham: Open University Press) is a useful compilation of research on leadership and team building geared towards early years practice.

Elliott, J. (1998) *The Curriculum Experiment: Meeting the Challenge of Social Change* (Buckingham: Open University Press) concludes with a chapter entitled 'What have we learnt from action research?' Elliott is one of the leading proponents of teacher-led curricular and pedagogic change in the UK and in this chapter draws on the work of Tony Giddens (1984) to discuss action research and the complex relationship between individual agency and organizational structures.

10 Early childhood services in the twenty-first century

Policy changes

In their book *Transforming Nursery Education*, Moss and Penn (1996) promoted a forward-looking vision of integrated services for young children and their families. At the end of the book they describe three versions of how workplaces might look in the twenty-first century: a community centre nursery, a school campus, and a nursery school and out-of-school club set in a park. These examples are illustrative of Moss and Penn's vision of 'a comprehensive, integrated and coherent early childhood service, flexible and multi-functional ... a rich and enhancing experience for everyone involved in it – children first and foremost, but also parents, staff, members of the local community' (p. 165).

Much of this vision is reflected in the policy initiatives in the UK for reshaping children's services outlined in Chapter 1. Of particular relevance to early childhood communities is the programme to develop *children's centres* offering integrated services for under-5s and their families at the hub of every community. There is also an expectation that through the *extended school* agenda networks of schools will play a central role in coordinating services for all children. What are the challenges embedded in this radical agenda for professionals working with young children? What are they expected to actually do? How will their daily working lives be changed?

Children's centres are charged with providing core services for babies and pre-school children including: good quality early learning integrated with full daycare (minimum ten hours per day, five days per week, 48 weeks per year); good quality teacher input to lead the development of learning within each centre; parental outreach and family support services; a base for training childminders and other childcare providers; child and family health services, including antenatal services; support for children with additional needs and their parents; and effective links with local adult education/training providers. By March 2006, within the first phase, children's centres will have reached 65 per cent of children in the most disadvantaged areas of England. Many Sure Start Local Programmes will have been expected to translate themselves into children's centres as their generous funding runs out in 2006. It is intended that children's centres' services are on a single site, close to a primary school. Early learning integrated with full daycare provision must be in the same building, but where services are delivered from more that one site, buildings must be within pram-pushing distance. It is expected that local authorities will work closely with the private sector in raising capital to extend childcare as children's centre provision is extended. Childminder networks are also encouraged to use children's centres, enabling them to network with health, family support and other professionals, as well as to access toy libraries, meeting rooms and joint training sessions.

Extended Schools, both mainstream and special schools, operate as hubs for services for school-aged pupils and their parents. New services may include: high-quality wraparound childcare, on the school site or with transfer arrangements to other local providers, available 8a.m.–6p.m. all year; a varied menu of activities in out of school hours to include homework clubs and study support, sport (at least two hours a day for those who want it), music, arts and crafts, dance, drama, special interest clubs (such as chess or first aid), visits to museums and galleries, learning a foreign language, volunteering, business and enterprise activities; parenting support including information at transition points, parenting programmes and family learning opportunities; swift and easy referral to specialist professionals such as speech therapists, child and adolescent mental health services, behaviour support and sexual health services. Some of these activities may be delivered on site. Children with disabilities or special educational needs must be able to access all new services. Extended schools are also charged with sharing access to ICT, sports and arts facilities with the local community, including adult learners.

The first challenge for the professionals who are implementing this radical policy agenda is to sustain the quality of services whilst reshaping them. We discussed in Chapters 1 and 2 the complexities of defining and measuring quality in traditional pre-school education, childcare and family support services and of taking into account the different views of stakeholders – inspectors, managers, practitioners, parents and children. There is increasing interest in listening to the voices of young children in defining and monitoring the quality of children's services (for example see Clark and Moss 2001). One of the remits of the newly appointed Children's Commissioner in England is to build up a repertoire of approaches to serious participation for children, when children and young people themselves are engaged in shaping decisions about services. A further complexity is the expectation that high-quality services for children under 5 are delivered in many different types of settings, each with their own histories and traditions – family centres, pre-school playgroups, private daycare chains, extended schools, child-minders' homes and Sure Start children's centres. Professionals will also be charged with providing (or brokering access to) a much wider range of services for children of school age (in England from the age of 4) and their parents, while ensuring that the services offered under their name are of the best possible quality. All these demands will create a sea change for the work of professionals charged with delivering early years services.

The new Ofsted inspection framework in England will be administered with a shorter, sharper focus on the Children Act *Five Outcomes* for children to be healthy, stay safe, enjoy and achieve, make a positive contribution and achieve economic well-being. The framework has a common set of characteristics for inspections across all phases of education, from early childhood to 19. But probably more significantly for professionals within learning networks, a greater emphasis will be accorded to self-evaluation. It may be that professionals have to work hard at establishing shared criteria for what constitutes quality in settings where multi-agency team work, rather than discipline specific practice, is central to service delivery. Criteria for what constitutes good quality in a service may look very different to a play worker, speech therapist, health visitor or teacher. It may also be important to acknowledge and resolve issues where the needs and demands of adults and children for services may sometimes be in tension. So, for example, in evaluating the quality of multi-disciplinary, innovative services for children under 4 and their families established under the auspices of Sure Start Local Programmes, the National Evaluation of Sure Start (NESS) team designed an innovative self-evaluation framework for centres delivering integrated early learning, play and childcare services (Anning *et al.* 2005). The domains of the characteristics include Principles and Shared Understandings, Good Practice in Service Delivery and Responding to the Community (for details see:www.surestart.gov.uk).

A further challenge is to improve the golden triangle of curriculum/pedagogy/assessment in promoting young children's learning. It is proving a challenge to implement the *Birth to Three Matters* and statutory Foundation Stage Curriculum across the wide range of settings attended by under-5s in England. Both the EPPE and NESS findings indicated that the quality of learning activities for young children were sometimes ill matched to their capabilities, either too formal and 'school-like' or too trite and undemanding, and in either case often presented to the children as inappropriate worksheet-based activities. In some settings there was little emphasis on children's cognitive development, with insufficient emphasis on informed ways of stimulating very young children's learning.

Practitioners seem confused about planning. Should they plan activities in advance to 'ensure' the delivery of the statutory Foundation Stage, or observe and document children's learning and plan from this evidence to extend children's learning, as in the much admired Reggio Emilia approach? They are also uncertain about assessment and record keeping. Should they just complete the detailed 13 assessment scales, each with 9 points, of the English Foundation Stage Profile? Or should they create learning stories for individual children as in the New Zealand model of assessment? Finally, there is little research evidence to help professionals understand the pedagogical principles of promoting the cognitive, emotional and social development of very young children, while acknowledging the role of adults in promoting their learning. The EPPE research cited in Chapters 2 and 4 gives us a starting point. But we remain concerned that, since we wrote the first edition of this book there has been so little research on the pedagogy of play, the pedagogy of early literacy and mathematical development, or the pedagogy of working with children under 3.

In order to back up the changes we have just outlined, English local authorities are required to adapt their local structures and systems to ensure that children's services, and the agencies responsible for their delivery, work in close partnership, sharing databases and delivering services within multi-professional teams. However, research in the field has indicated that it takes a long time for professionals from different disciplines and agencies to learn to work together effectively. For example, research for the Multi-Agency Team work for Children's Services (MATCh) project (Anning *et al.* 2006) based at Leeds University into five 'successful' multi-agency teams found that professionals had to negotiate transformations in their identities as specialists (sometimes of high status) working with clients in ways previously determined by their training and work experiences in single agency contexts, to identities as generic workers with team responsibilities for activities with clients. In order to function effectively, team members had to acknowledge the pain of the destabilization of some professionals' specialist identities in the workplace. It took a long time for professionals to tune into each other's ways of working with and talking about clients.

Where conflicts in differing beliefs, values and approaches to treatments were acknowledged, confronted and reconciled between the team members, teams were able to move on positively to new ways of working. Where conflicts were suppressed, dealt with on the basis of 'status' knowledge (for example that of a pediatrician versus a family worker), power (for example a voluntary agency manager versus a local authority officer) or personalities (and this was sometimes related to gender) rather than rationalizing working practices in the best interests of clients, or resolved by high-handed managerial decisions, teams foundered. It was important for team members to nurture the team as a whole, while at the same time supporting individual members who were going through changes in their working practices which could make them feel uncomfortable or insecure (see Anning *et al.* 2006). Once they had struggled through the pain barriers of coping with changes in their roles and responsibilities, many professionals acknowledged how much they had learned from working in integrated service settings. However, we have little robust research evidence so far of the impact of multi-agency service delivery on users. It may be that while complex structural and systematic changes towards integrated service delivery are being implemented by the professionals, users are receiving less targeted (and less effective?) treatment from highly qualified professionals than they did under the single agency models of service delivery.

The biggest resource we have for taking forward innovation are the professionals charged with making the vision of integrated children's services a reality. As we have seen already in discussing the specifics of the project reported in this book, there is a complex relationship between organization structures and individual agency. But for workers to be agentic in their practice, they need to be well-informed and confident. The government is facing an uphill struggle to redress the years of under-funding of the professional workforce for young children. The Labour Force Survey of 2003 showed that only 12 per cent of childcare and early years workers are qualified to Level 4 (graduate status) in the UK qualifications listings and almost 40 per cent are not qualified even to Level 2.

A new concept of the *early years professional* is to be developed in the UK. S/he may be a 'new' teacher trained to work across care and education settings from birth to 16, or a pedagogue of graduate status trained to work across the sectors of care, learning and health. Key elements of the UK government agenda for building a world-class workforce in young children's services include an early years professional in all 3,500 planned children's centres by 2010, in every full daycare setting by 2015 and, as a longer term vision, in every Foundation Stage setting. These proposals have profound implications for the training of teachers to work in early years settings. A Children's Workforce Development Council is charged with developing a generic qualification framework for all professionals working with children with transferable units of core and specialist skills and knowledge. New employers will be expected to invest in training in additional specialist skills for their workforce. In order to fund the rising levels of pay, which will parallel the raising of the qualifications and status of children's services professionals, the ten-year strategy for childcare has included a transformation fund of

£125 million per year. There will also be renewed attempts to increase the number of male workers in early years services (see Cameron *et al.* 1999).

Finally, the UK government has recognized the complex challenges of managing and leading settings through a period of change. It is now acknowledged that managers of children's centres in England will need to be trained in the ability to lead and manage change, including responsibilities for staffing, capital builds and large budgets. There is a national graduate training scheme, pioneered at the Pen Green Centre, called the National Professional Qualification in Integrated Centre Leadership. All managers of children's centres will be required to gain this qualification. This initiative will be pivotal to achieving sustainable, systematic change in integrated children's services.

Policy into practice: working towards a community of understanding

Policy changes at the outer, macro-level, of systems can seem oppressive to those struggling to implement them at the micro-level of their workplaces. Yet Bronfenbrenner's model (Bronfenbrenner 1979; Bronfenbrenner and Ceci 1994) allocates to both children and the adults working with them an active role in shaping their own practices and behaviours within the various levels so that they in turn can impact from the inside outwards and infuence policy makers. Certainly taking a proactive rather than reactive stance in managing change makes workers feel less like the victims of circumstances beyond their control. But, as we have argued, practitioners need support at critical times to enable them to face up to and manage change.

The model we adopted in the project reported in this book was to set up cross-professional and cross-authority learning networks in the exo- and meso-systems surrounding the practitioners' workplaces (see Chapter 1). We learned how important these networks were to sustain the momentum for change, providing opportunities for conversations about practice, underpinned by theory and research evidence. It is hard for practitioners to persevere at analysis of their practice in their own workplaces without the incentive of sympathetic listeners, feedback gained from sharing their ideas with critical but informed others and reassurance that their work is valued. We were working towards establishing a community of understanding of informed professionals which would survive the immediate aims of the project. In fact, not only did these networks sustain innovation during the project but also they led to sub-groups forming and re-forming for secondary professional purposes within the local authorities. In some cases the support systems have encouraged individuals to change career aspirations or study for degree- or Masters-level qualifications. So the aspiration to influence others out there beyond the micro-system level has been realized by members of the project networking beyond their workplace boundaries.

A second crucial principle was that face-to-face interactions between members of the community of understanding was based on documentary evidence of the realities of their everyday working lives. The action research model provided a demanding but rewarding structure by which we were all required to centre our conversations on analysis of observations, field notes, photographs, video recordings, children's models and drawings and the conversations of parents and staff. Only by focusing on these realities and developing a culture of collaboration which included challenge without confrontation could we move forward and begin to develop a discourse of informed practice that bridged the gaps we encountered between the working realities and priorities of the university, daycare, playgroup, school and childminding worlds.

It became increasingly obvious that we needed to bridge another gap – that between practitioners and parents. We learnt that it was often through discussing cultural tools (children's drawings, scrapbooks, profile notes) when engaging parents in dialogue about their children that we began to recognize the significance of these objects as the stimuli for meaningful exchanges. In contrast, formal meetings set up to transmit 'professional knowledge' to parents or 'parenting programmes' based on the assumptions that their parenting was somehow deficit, often foundered.

We learnt that communication across all manner of gaps was at a deep rather than superficial level if it recognized rather than repressed differences in people's views of children and their needs and used the differences as the creative starting point for meaningful exchanges of ideas. We were all catapulted outside our own safe worlds of work both literally and metaphorically. For some practitioners, coming into a university workplace setting for meetings was intimidating, and for the researchers complex journeys across three large local authority areas in search of day care or nursery workplace settings forced them to confront anxieties of their own about how they would cope with unfamiliar people and places. Many of us were juggling domestic with professional responsibilities. We all stepped out of domestic realities into living together in the unfamiliar surroundings of a hotel and a hall of residence for two residentials. None of this was easy. It required taking risks and risking loss of face for every one of the project team at some point as we worked together to co-construct our community of understanding.

A knowledge base for early years professionals

Project members came from a range of different types of settings. The foci for sharing our knowledge as practitioners in this project were literacy and mathematical thinking, but the skills we acquired in researching and making explicit what knowledge we carried within our practice were transferable to other areas of learning. We could have gained as much from focusing on knowledge and understanding of the world or on creative activities, for example. An important principle was that it was the starting point of analysing episodes of children and adults learning together in real settings that gave our dialogues authenticity and depth. When we tracked episodes of literacy and mathematical learning in settings, there was evidence that much valuable learning was happening within the everyday activities of the daily play and domestic routines. It came as a surprise to many of the group that there was so much wisdom in their current often intuitive practice. Careful analysis of those episodes prompted us to want to make much more of what we were already doing. So, for example, practitioners did not want to buy expensive new equipment or resources but they wanted to make much better informed use of what they already had. Over and over again we came to the realization that though we were apparently planning activities competently, we were less certain about the quality of adult and children's learning behaviours when our paper plans were translated into actions.

Sometimes the hardest task was to put our implicit knowledge into words. Project members groaned at our requests that they write down what they had learned from their action research in order to make that knowledge explicit for a wider audience. However, having once grasped the nettle, at our last residential together, the team were adamant when they reviewed the accumulated papers outlining the individual projects, that they wanted to publish accounts of the research and analysis they had done. As they rightly argued, others reading their guidelines for literacy and mathematical thinking for young children would need to understand the processes by which they had come to their curriculum models. They did not want to publish a set of 'tips' for practitioners.

To their great credit, though they expressed clearly at the start of the project that they were less confident in their grasp of mathematical learning, many of the team took the risk of focusing on mathematics for their action research cycle. By the end of the project the repertory grid exercise indicated that though they still felt less confident in their grasp of mathematics than literacy learning, nevertheless they had developed a greater 'at homeness' with number. Their confidence in managing children's learning in literacy had developed considerably. Though putting what they knew in writing had been demanding, they acknowledged that it had helped them to clarify their own understanding. When we shared all the project materials at the final residential they gained confidence from the realization that their professional knowledge both as individuals and as a community was impressive. Thus in articulating their understanding of how children learnt, they had themselves taken great strides as adult learners.

Again and again we returned to the notion of the significance of the quality of interactions between adults and children and adults and adults in the workplace as at the heart and soul of good professional practice. A phrase that had initially seemed abstract and intimidating to the group, 'joint involvement episodes', became a kind of mantra for the team when we focused on the 'pedagogy' of working with young children. We also recognized the importance of the degree of intimacy and emotional engagement between adults and children if they were to be meaningful to both parties. We recognized the importance of structuring high-quality learning opportunities – sharing books, setting up lively construction play areas, making music, making meaning through art work, models or role-play. But we became more and more convinced of the importance of adults following children's learning by careful observation as the precursor to leading children, through guided participation, towards new learning. Yet, as we have argued, early years professionals and researchers need to substantiate this approach with robust research evidence to counter the 'colonization' of home and pre-school settings by inappropriate educational dogma.

Our hope is that the kind of collaboration between higher education-based researchers, local authority officers and early years professionals exemplified in the project on which this book was based will fire others with enthusiasm and intellectual curiosity to explore the complexity within the daily lives of young children and the adults who love, work and play with them. Only by those who care explaining to others how it is will the world of early childhood come to be valued as it should be.

Bibliography

Abbott, L. and Moylett, H. (eds) (1997a) *Working with Under-threes: Training and Professional Development.* Buckingham: Open University Press.

Abbott, L. and Moylett, H. (eds) (1997b) *Working with Under-threes: Responding to Children's Needs.* Buckingham: Open University Press.

Anning, A. (1994) Play and the legislated curriculum: back to basics, an alternative view, in J. Moyles (ed.) (1994) *The Excellence of Play.* Buckingham: Open University Press.

Anning, A. (1997) *First Years at School.* 2nd edn Buckingham: Open University Press.

Anning, A. (1999) Learning to draw and drawing to learn, *Journal of Art and Design Education*, 18 (2): 163–72.

Anning, A. (2002) Conversations around young children's drawing: the impact of the beliefs of significant others at home and school, *Journal of Art and Design Education*, 21 (3): 197–219.

Anning, A. (2005a) Investigating the impact of working in multi-agency service delivery settings in the UK on early years practitioners' beliefs and practices, *Journal of Early Childhood Research*. Vol 3 (1): 19–50.

Anning, A. (2005b) Play and the legislated curriculum: back to basics, and alternative view, in J. Moyles (ed.) *The Excellence of Play.* 2nd edn Maidenhead: Open University/McGraw-Hill Education.

Anning, A., Chesworth, E. and Spurling, L. (2005) *The Quality of Early Learning, Play and Childcare Service in Sure Start Local Programmes.* London: National Evaluation of Sure Start at Birkbeck College and Department of Education and Skills.

Anning, A., Cottrell, D., Frost, N., Green, J. and Robinson, M. (2006, forthcoming) *Developing Multiprofessional Teamwork for Integrated Children's Services.* Maidenhead: Open University Press/McGraw-Hill Education.

Anning, A., Cullen, J. and Fleer, M. (2004) *Early Childhood Education: Society and Culture.* London: Sage.

Anning, A. and Ring, K. (2004) *Making Sense of Children's Drawings.* Maidenhead: Open University Press/McGraw-Hill Education.

Arnett, J. (1989) Care-givers in daycare centres: Does training matter? *Journal of Applied Psychology*, 10 (4): 541–52.

Athey, C. (1990) *Extending Thought in Young Children: A Parent-Teacher Partnership.* London: Paul Chapman.

Atkinson, M., Wilkin, A., Stott, A., Doherty, P. and Kinder, K. (2002) *Multi-agency Working: A Detailed Study.* Slough: National Foundation for Educational Research.

Aubrey, C. (1996) An investigation of teachers' mathematical subject knowledge and processes of instruction in reception classes, *British Educational Research Journal*, 22 (2): 181–97.

Aubrey, C. (1997a) *Mathematics Teaching in the Early Years*. London: Falmer.

Aubrey, C. (1997b) Children's early learning of number in school and out, in I. Thompson (ed.) *Teaching and Learning Early Number*. Buckingham: Open University Press.

Aubrey, C., Bottle, G. and Godfrey, R. (2003) Early mathematics in the home and out-of-home contexts, *International Journal of Early Years Education*, 11 (2): 91–103.

Audit Commission (1997) *Counting to Five*. Abingdon: Audit Commission Publications.

Baghban, M. (1984) *Our Daughter Learns to Read and Write*. Newark, DE: International Reading Association.

Ball, C. (1994) *Start Right: The Importance of Early Learning*. London: Royal Society of Arts.

Barnes, J., Broomfield, K., Dave, S., Frost, M., Melhuish, E. and Belsky, J. (2004) *Disadvantaged but Different: Variation in Deprived Communities in Relation to Child and Family Well-being*. National Evaluation of Sure Start. London: NESS, Birkbeck College for DfES Sure Start Unit (www.dfes.gov.uk).

Baroody, A.J. (1987) *Children's Mathematical Thinking*. New York: Teachers College Press.

Baroody, A.J. (1993) Fostering the mathematical learning of young children, in B. Spodeck (ed.) *Handbook of Research on the Education of Young Children*. New York: Macmillan.

Baroody, A.J. (2000) Does mathematics instruction for three to five-year-olds really make sense? *Young Children*, July, 61–7.

Belsky, J. (1999) International and contextual determinants of attachment security, in J. Cassidy and P.R. Shaver (eds) *Handbook of Attachment: Theory, Research and Clinical Applications*. New York: Guildford: 249–64.

Bennett, N. and Kell, J. (1989) *A Good Start: Four Year Olds in Infant Schools*. Oxford: Basil Blackwell.

Bennett, N., Wood, E. and Rogers, S. (1997) *Teaching Through Play: Reception Teachers' Theories and Practice*. Buckingham: Open University Press.

Berg, L. (1977) *Reading and hearing*. London: Routledge and Kegan Paul.

Berliner, D. and Calfee, R. (eds) (1996) *Handbook of Educational Psychology*. New York: Macmillan.

Bertram, A. and Pascal, C. (1999) *Early Excellence Centres: Developing High Quality Integrated Early Years Services: First Findings*. Nottingham: Department for Education and Employment.

Bertram, A. and Pascal, C. (2001) *Early Excellence Centres Pilot Programme Annual Evaluation Report.* London: DfEE.

Bertram, A., Pascal, C., Bokhari, S., Gasper, M., Holtermann, S. (2002) *Early Excellence Pilot Programme: Second Evaluation Report 2002–2001. Research Report RR361.* Norwich: HMSO.

Bissex, G.L. (1980) *GNYS AT WRK: A Child Learns to Read and Write.* London: Harvard University Press.

Blenkin, G. and Hutchin, V. (1998) Action research, child observations and professional development: some evidence from a research project, *Early Years*, 19 (1) (Autumn): 62–75.

Blenkin, G. and Kelly, A.V. (eds) (1997) *Principles into Practice in Early Childhood Education.* London: Paul Chapman.

Book Trust (1998) *A Gift For Life: Bookstart, Fifth Year.* London: Book Trust.

Bowlby, J. (1953) *Child Care and the Growth of Love.* Harmondsworth: Penguin.

Bradley, M. (1982) *The Coordination of Services for Children Under Five.* Windsor: NFER/Nelson.

Briggs, R. (1969) *The Mother Goose Treasury.* London: Hamish Hamilton.

Bronfenbrenner, U. (1979) *The Ecology of Human Development: Experiments by Nature and Design.* Cambridge, MA: Harvard University Press.

Bronfenbrenner, U. and Ceci, S.J. (1994) Nature nurture reconceptualized in Developmental Perspective: A Bioecological Model. *Psychological Review.* NO. 101 (4): 568–86.

Brooks, G., Gorman, T., Harman, J., Hutchison, D. and Wilkin, A. (1996) *Family Literacy Works: The NFER Evaluation of the Basic Skills Agency's Demonstration Programmes.* London: Basic Skills Agency.

Bruner, J.S. (1963) *The Process of Education.* New York: Vintage.

Bruner, J.S. (1983) *Child's Talk: Learning to Use Language.* Oxford: Oxford University Press.

Bruner, J.S. (1996) *The Culture of Education.* Cambridge, MA: Harvard University Press.

Burton, L. (2002) Children's mathematical narratives as learning stories, *European Early Childhood Education Research Journal,* 10 (2): 5–18.

Cameron, C., Moss, P., and Owen, C. (1999) *Men in the Nursery: Gender and Caring Work.* London: Paul Chapman Publishing.

Campbell, R. (1996) *Literacy in Nursery Education*, Stoke-on-Trest: Trentham Books.

Campbell, R. and Olson, D. (1990) Children's thinking, in R. Grieve and M. Hughes (eds) *Understanding Children.* Oxford: Blackwell.

Carr, M. (2001) *Assessment in Early Years Settings: Learning Stories.* London: Paul Chapman Publishing.

Carr, M. and Claxton, G. (2002) Tracking the development of learning dispositions, *Assessment in Education,* 9 (1): 93–7. In H. Daniels and A. Edwards (eds) (2004) *The RoutledgeFalmer Reader in Psychology of Education.* London: RoutledgeFalmer.

Chaiklin, S. (2004) The zone of proximal development in Vygotsky's analysis of learning and instruction, in A. Kozulin, B. Gindis, V. Ageyev and S. Miller (eds) *Vygotsky's Educational Theory in Cultural Context.* Cambridge: Cambridge University Press.

Chaiklin, S. and Lave, J. (eds) (1993) *Understanding Practice: Perspectives on Activity and Context.* Cambridge: Cambridge University Press.

Chomsky, N. (1976) *Reflections on Language.* London: Fontana.

Clark, A. and Moss, P. (2001) *Listening to Young Children: the Mosaic Approach.* London: Paul Chapman Publishing.

Claxton, G. and Carr, M. (2004) A framework for teaching learning: the dynamics of disposition, *Early Years,* 24 (1): 87–97.

Clay, M. (1975) *What Did I Write?* London: Heinemann Educational Books.

Cleave, S. and Brown, S. (1989) *Meeting their Needs.* Windsor: NFER/ Nelson.

Cleave, S. and Brown, S. (1991a) *Four Year Olds in Infant Classes.* Windsor: NFER/ Nelson.

Cleave, S. and Brown, S. (1991b) *Quality Matters.* Windsor: NFER/Nelson.

Clements, D. (2002) Computers in early mathematics, *Contemporary Issues in Early Childhood,* 3 (2): 160–81.

Cockcroft, W.H. (1982) *Mathematics Counts: Report of the Committee of Enquiry into the Teaching of Mathematics in Schools.* London: HMSO.

Cole, M. (1996) *Cultural Psychology.* Cambridge MA: Harvard University Press.

Cole, M., Engestrom, Y. and Vasquez, O. (eds) (1997) *Mind, Culture and Activity.* Cambridge: Cambridge University Press.

Cooter, R. (ed.) (1992) *In the Name of the Child.* London: Routledge.

Cope, B. and Kalantzis, M. (eds) (2000) *Multi-literacies: Literary Learning and the Design of Social Futures.* London: Routledge.

Cullen, J. (2001) Ethics and assessment in early childhood programmes. *Early Education,* 27 (Spring–Summer): 5–11.

Dahlberg, G., Moss, P. and Pearce, A. (1999) *Beyond Quality in Early Childhood Education and Care: Postmodern Perspectives.* London: Falmer Press.

Daniels, H. and Edwards, A. (eds) (2004) *The RoutledgeFalmer Reader in Psychology of Education.* London: RoutledgeFalmer.

David, T. (ed.) (1993) *Educational Provision for our Youngest Children.* London: Paul Chapman.

David, T. (ed.) (1998) *Researching Early Childhood Education: European Perspectives.* London: Paul Chapman.

De Corte, E., Greer, B. and Verschaffel, L. (1996) Mathematics teaching and learning, in D. Berliner and R. Calfee (eds) *Handbook of Educational Psychology*. New York: Macmillan.

DES (Department of Education and Science) (1988) *National Curriculum Task Group on Assessment and Testing: A Report*. London: HMSO.

Desforges, C. (1995) How does experience affect theoretical knowledge for teaching? *Learning and Instruction*, 5 (4): 385–400.

DfEE (Department for Education and Employment) (1997) *Excellence in Schools*. London: HMSO.

DfEE (Department for Education and Employment) (1998a) *Meeting the Childcare Challenge* (Green Paper). London: HMSO.

DfEE (Department for Education and Employment) (1998b) *The National Literacy Strategy: Framework for Teaching*. London: DfEE.

DfEE (Department of Education and Employment) (1998c) *The Implementation of the National Numeracy Strategy: the Final Report of the Numeracy Task Force*. London: DfEE.

DfEE (Department for Education and Employment) (1999a) *Early Years Development Partnerships and Plans: Guidance 1998–99*. London: DfEE.

DfEE (Department for Education and Employment) (1999b) *Teachers Meeting the Challenge of Change* (Green Paper), Cm 4164. London: HMSO.

DfEE (Department for Education and Employment) (2001a) *Early Years Development and Childcare Planning Guidance 2001–02*. Nottingham: DfEE Publications.

DfEE (Department for Education and Employment) (2001b) *Early Excellence Centres: Developing High Quality Integrated Services*. London: DfEE.

DfEE/QCA (2000) *Curriculum Guidance for the foundation stage*. Qualification and Curriculum Authority: London.

DfEE/SCAA (Department for Education and Employment/School Curriculum and Assessment Authority) (1996) *Desirable Outcomes for Children's Learning on Entering Compulsory Education*. London: DfEE/SCAA.

DfES (Department for Education and Skills) (1990) *Starting with Quality: Report of the Committee on Enquiry into the Quality of Educational Experiences Offered to 3- and 4-year-olds*. London: HMSO.

DfES (Department for Education and Skills) (2002) *Birth to Three Matters: A Framework for Supporting Children in their Earliest Years*. London: DfES.

DfES (Department for Education and Skills) (2004) *Every Child Matters: The Next Steps*. Green Paper. London: HMSO.

DfES (Department for Education and Skills) (2005) *Ten Year Strategy for Childcare*. London: HMSO.

Dijk, E., van Oers, B. and Terwel, J. (2004) Schematising in early childhood mathematics education: why, when and how? *European Early Childhood Education Research Journal,* 12 (1): 71–83.

DoH (Department of Health) (1991) *The Children Act 1989: Guidance and Regulations, Volume 2, Day Care and Educational Provision for Young Children.* London: HMSO.

Donaldson, M. (1978) *Children's Minds.* London: Croom Helm.

Dowling, M. (2005) *Young Children's Social and Emotional Development,* Second Edition. London: Paul Chapman Publishing.

Drummond, M.J. (1993) *Assessing Children's Learning.* London: David Fulton.

Dunn, J. (1988) *The Beginnings of Social Understanding.* Oxford: Blackwell.

Dunn, J. (2005) Relationships and children's discovery of mind, British Academy/British Psychological Society Annual Lecture, London, 2005.

Early Childhood Forum (1998) *Quality in Diversity in Early Learning: A Framework for Early Childhood Practitioners.* London: National Children's Bureau.

Easen, P., Atkins, M. and Dyson, A. (2000) Inter-professional collaboration and conceptualisations of practice. *Children and Society,* 14: 335–67.

Edwards, A. (1998) Mentoring student teachers in primary schools, *European Journal of Teacher Education,* 21 (1): 47–62.

Edwards, A. (1999) Research and practice: is there a dialogue? in H. Penn (ed.) *Theory, Policy and Practice in Early Childhood Services.* Buckingham: Open University Press.

Edwards, A. (2001) Qualitative designs and analysis, in G. MacNaughton, S. Rolfe and I. Siraj-Blatchford (eds) *Doing Early Childhood Research: theory and practice an international perspective.* Buckingham: Open University Press.

Edwards, A. (2004a) The new multi-agency working: collaborating to prevent the social exclusion of children and families, *Journal of Integrated Care,* 12 (5): 3–9.

Edwards, A. (2004b) Understanding context, understanding practice in early education, *European Early Childhood Education Research Journal,* 12 (1): 85–101.

Edwards, A. (2005) Let's get beyond community and practice: the many meanings of learning by participating, *The Curriculum Journal,* 16 (1): 49–65.

Edwards, A. and Brunton, D. (1993) Supporting reflection in teachers' learning, in J. Calderhead and P. Gates (eds) *Conceptualising Reflection in Teacher Development.* London: Falmer.

Edwards, A. and Talbot, R. (1999) *The Hardpressed Researcher: A Research Handbook for Education, Health and Social Care,* 2nd edn. London: Longman.

Edwards, C., Gandini, L. and Forman, G. (eds) (1993) *The Hundred*

Languages of Children: The Reggio Emilia Approach to Early Childhood Education. Norwood: NJ: Ablex Publishing Company.

Egan, K. (1988) *Primary Understanding: Education in Early Childhood*. London: Routledge.

Elfer, P., Goldschmied, E. and Selleck, D. (1999) *Working with Children Under Three: The Keyperson Relationship*. London: National Children's Bureau.

Elfer, P., Goldschmeid, E. and Selleck, D. (2003) *Key Person Relationships in Nursery*. London: Sage.

Elliott, J. (1994) Research on teachers' knowledge in action research, *Educational Action Research*, 2 (1): 133–7.

Elliott, J. (1998) *The Curriculum Experiment: Meeting the Challenge of Social Change*. Buckingham: Open University Press.

Engeström, Y. (1993) Developmental studies of work as a testbench of activity theory: the case of primary care medical practice, in S. Chaiklin and J. Lave (eds) *Understanding Practice: Perspectives on Activity and Context*. Cambridge: Cambridge University Press.

Engeström, Y. (1999) Activity theory and individual and social transformation, in Y. Engeström, R. Miettinen and R-L. Punamäki (eds) *Perspectives on Activity Theory*. Cambridge: Cambridge University Press.

Ferreiro, E. and Teberovsky, A. (1982) *Literacy Before Schooling*. London: Heinemann Educational Books.

Ferri, E., Birchall, D., Gingell, V. and Gipps, C. (1981) *Combined Nursery Centres: A New Approach to Education and Day Care*. London: Macmillan.

Fransella, F. and Bannister, D. (1977) *A Manual for Repertory Grid Technique*. New York: Academic Press.

Fransella, F. and Thomas, L. (eds) (1988) *Experimenting with Personal Construct Psychology*. London: Routledge.

Frith, U. (1989) *Autism: Explaining the Enigma*. Oxford: Blackwell.

Fromberg, D.P. (1990) An agenda for research on play in early childhood education, in E. Klugman and S. Smilansky (eds) *Children's Play and Learning: Policy Implications*. New York: Columbia University Teachers College Press.

Fullan, M. (1991) *The New Meaning of Educational Change*. London: Cassell.

Fullan, M. (1993) *Change Forces*. London: Falmer.

Fuson, K. and Hall, J. (1983) The acquisition of early number word meanings: a conceptual analysis and review, in H. Ginsburg (ed.) *The Development of Mathematical Thinking*. New York: Academic Press.

Gelman, R. and Gallistel, C.R. (1986) *The Child's Understanding of Number*. Cambridge, MA: Harvard University Press.

Gifford, S. (2004) Between the secret garden and the hothouse: children's responses to number focused activities in the nursery, *European Early Childhood Research Journal,* 12 (2): 87–102.

Ginsburg, H. (ed.) (1983) *The Development of Mathematical Thinking.* New York: Academic Press.

Gipps, C. (1994) *Beyond Testing: Towards a Theory of Educational Assessment.* London: Falmer.

Goldschmied, E. and Jackson, S. (1994) *People Under Three.* London: Routledge.

Goldstein, L. (1999) The relational zone: the role of caring relationships in the co-construction of mind, *American Educational Research Journal,* 36 (3): 647–73.

Goleman, D. (1996) *Emotional Intelligence.* London: Bloomsbury.

Goswami, U. and Bryant, P.E. (1990) *Phonological Skills and Learning to Read.* London: Lawrence Erlbaum Associates.

Gregory, E. (1996) *Making Sense of a New World: Learning to Read in a Second Language.* London: Paul Chapman.

Gregory, E. (ed.) (1997) *One Child, Many Worlds: Early Learning in Multicultural Communities.* London: David Fulton Publishers.

Gregory, E. (ed.) (1998) *One Child, Many Worlds: Early Learning in Multicultural Communities.* London: David Fulton Publishers.

Harms, T., Clifford, R. and Cryer, B. (1998) *Early Childhood Environment Ratings Scales and Infant Toddler Environment Ratings Scales.* New York and London: Teachers' College Press.

Harré, R. (1983) *Personal Being.* Oxford: Blackwell.

Hawkins, P. and Shohet, R. (1989) *Supervision in the Helping Professions.* Buckingham: Open University Press.

Hayes, C.D., Palmer, J.L. and Zaslow, M. (1990) *Who Cares for America's Children.* Washington D.C.: National Academy Press.

Heath, S.B. (1982) What no bedtime story means: narrative skills at home and at school, *Language in Society,* 11: 49–75.

Heath, S.B. (1983) *Ways with Words: Language, Life and Work in Communities and Classrooms.* Cambridge: Cambridge University Press.

Henessy, E., Martin, S., Moss, P. and Melhuish, E. (1992) *Children and Daycare: Lessons from Research.* London: Paul Chapman Publishing.

Hirst, P. (1996) The demands of professional practice and preparation for teaching, in J. Furlong and R. Smith (eds) *The Role of Higher Education in Initial Teacher Training.* London: Kogan Page.

HMSO Education, Arts and Science Committee (1989) *Achievement in Primary Schools,* Vol. 1. London: HMSO.

HMSO (1998) Meeting the Childcare Challenge. London: HMSO.

HMSO (2004) *Reading for Purpose and Pleasure: An Evaluation of the Teaching of Reading in Primary Schools.* London: Ofsted Publications Centre.

HMSO (2005) *Teaching Children to Read, Eighth Report of Session 2004-2005. House of Commons Education and Skills Committee.* London: DfES.

Holtermann, S. (1992) *Investing in Young Children: Costing an Education and Day Care Service.* London: National Children's Bureau.

Holtermann, S. (1995) *Investing in Young Children: A Reassessment of the Cost of an Education and Day Care Service.* London: National Children's Bureau.

Hopkins, D. (1993) *A Teachers' Guide to Classroom Research,* 2nd edn Buckingham: Open University Press.

House of Commons Education and Skills Committee (2005) *Teaching Children to Read, Eighth Report of the Session 2004-05,* HC 121, London: HMSO.

Huberman, M. (1995) Networks that alter teaching: conceptualisations, exchanges and experiments, *Teachers and Teaching: Theory and Practice,* 1 (2): 193-211.

James, A. and Prout, A. (1997) *Constructing and De-constructing Childhood.* London: Falmer.

Karmiloff, K. and Karmiloff-Smith, A. (2001) *Pathways to Language: from Foetus to Adolescent.* Cambridge, MA: Harvard University Press.

Kleinburg, S. and Menmuir, J. (1995) Perceptions of mathematics in prefives settings, *Education,* 3-13 (October): 29-35.

Konkola, R. (2001) Developmental process of internship at polytechnic and boundary zone activity as a new model for activity, in T. Tuomi-Gröhn and Y. Engeström (eds) *At the Boundary Zone between School and Work.* Helsinki: Helsinki University Press.

Kress, G. (1997) *Before Writing: Rethinking the Paths to Literacy.* London: Routledge.

Laevers, F. (ed.) (1994) *The Leuven Involvement Scale for Young Children.* Leuven, Belgium: Centre for Experiential Education.

Laminack, L. (1991) *Learning with Zachary.* Richmond Hill, Ontario: Scholastic Canada.

Lave, J. and Wenger, E. (1991) *Situated Learning: Legitimate Peripheral Participation.* Cambridge: Cambridge University Press.

Louis, K.S., Marks, H. and Kruse, S. (1996) Teachers' professional communities in restructuring schools, *American Educational Research Journal,* 33 (4): 757-98.

MacNaughton, G., Rolfe, S. and Siraj-Blatchford, I. (eds) (2001) *Doing Early Childhood Research: Theory and Practice an International Perspective.* Buckingham: Open University Press.

Makins, V. (1997) *Not Just a Nursery: Multi-agency Early Years Centres in Action.* London: National Children's Bureau.

Malaguzzi, L. (ed.) (1987) *I Cento Linguaggi dei Bambini [The Hundred Languages of Children] Assessorato all 'istuzione,* Reggio Emilia.

Marsh, J. (2004) The techno-literacy practices of young children, *Journal of Early Childhood Research*. Vol. 2 (1): 51–66.

Marsh, J. and Millard, E. (2000) *Literacy and Popular Culture: Using Children's Culture in the Classroom*. London: Paul Chapman Publishing.

Matterson, E. (1996) *This Little Puffin: Finger Play and Nursery Rhymes*. London: Puffin.

Matthews, J. (1994) *Helping Children to Draw and Paint in Early Childhood: Young Children and Visual Representation*. London: Hodder & Stoughton.

Meadows, S. (1993) *The Child as Thinker*. London: Routledge.

Meek, M. (1998) Important Reading Lessons, in B. Cox (ed.) *Literacy Is Not Enough*. Manchester: Manchester Book Trust: 116–23.

Melhuish, E.C. (1991) Research on day care for young children in the United Kingdom, in E.C. Melhuish and P. Moss (eds) *Day Care for Young Children: International Perspectives*. London: Routledge.

Melhuish, E.C. (2004) *Child Benefits: the Importance of Investing in Quality Childcare. Daycare Trust's Facing the Future Policy Paper No 9*. London: Daycare Trust.

Melhuish, E.C., Belsky, J., Ball, M. and Anning, A. (2005) Variation in Sure Start Level Programme Effectiveness. www.surestart.gov.uk.

Mercer, N. (1995) *The Guided Construction of Knowledge: Talk Amongst Teachers and Learners*. Clevedon: Multilingual Matters.

Mercer, N. (1996) The quality of children's collaborative talk in the classroom, *Learning and Instruction*, 6 (4): 359–77.

Mercer, N. (2000) *Words and Minds: how we use language to think together*. London: Routledge.

Merttens, R. and Vass, J. (1990) *Bringing School Home: Children and Parents Learning Together*. London: Hodder & Stoughton.

Merttens, R. and Vass, J. (eds) (1993) *Partnerships in Maths: Parents and School*. London: Falmer.

Miller, L. (1996) *Towards Reading*. Buckingham: Open University Press.

Miller, L. (2001) Shaping early childhood through the literacy curriculum, *Early Years* 2 (2): 107–16.

Mills, C. and Mills, D. (1998) *Britain's Early Years Disaster* (survey of research evidence for Channel 4 television documentary *Too Much, Too Soon*). London: Channel 4 Television.

MoE (Ministry of Education, New Zealand) (1993–96) *Te Whariki, He Whaariki Matauranga: Early Childhood Curriculum*. Wellington: New Zealand Learning Media.

MoE (Ministry of Education, New Zealand) (2002) *Pathways to the Future: Ng huarahi aratiki. A Ten Year Strategic Plan for Early Childhood Education*. Wellington: New Zealand Learning Media.

Montague-Smith, A. (1997) *Mathematics in Nursery Education*. London: David Fulton.

Moss, P. (1992) Perspectives from Europe, in G. Pugh (ed.) *Contemporary Issues in the Early Years*. London: Paul Chapman.

Moss, P. and Pence, A. (eds) (1994) *Valuing Quality in Early Childhood Services*. London: Paul Chapman.

Moss, P. and Penn, H. (1996) *Transforming Nursery Education*. London: Paul Chapman.

Muldoon, K., Lewis, C. and Freeman, N. (2003) Putting counting to work: preschoolers' understanding of cardinal extension, *International Journal of Educational Research*, 39: 695–718.

Munn, P. (1994a) Perceptions of teaching and learning in pre-school centres, in M. Hughes (ed.) *Perceptions of Teaching and Learning*. Clevedon: MultiLingual Matters.

Munn, P. (1994b) The early development of literacy and numeracy skills, *European Early Childhood Research Journal*, 2 (1): 5–18.

Munn, P. (1997a) Children's beliefs about counting, in I. Thompson (ed.) *Teaching and Learning Early Number*. Buckingham: Open University Press.

Munn, P. (1997b) Writing and number, in I. Thompson (ed.) *Teaching and Learning Early Number*. Buckingham: Open University Press.

Munn, P. and Schaffer, H.R. (1993) Literacy and numeracy events in social interactive contexts, *International Journal of Early Years Education*, 1 (3): 61–80.

Murray, L. and Andrews, E. (2000) *The Social Baby*. London: Richmond Press.

National Audit Office (2004) *Early Years: Progress in Developing High Quality Childcare and Early Education Accessible to All*. London: TSO. 50 pp.

National Commission on Education (1993) *Learning to Succeed: A Radical Look at Education Today and a Strategy for the Future*. London: Heinemann.

National Institute for Child Health and Human Development: Early Child Care Research Network (2004) Does amount of time spent in child care predict socio-emotional adjustment during the transition to kindergarten? *Child Development*. July/August 2003. Vol. 74 (4): 976–1005.

NECF (National Evaluation of Children's Funds) (2004) *Collaborating for the Social Inclusion of Children and Young People: emerging lessons from the first round of case studies*. London: DfES.

Newson, J. and Newson, E. (1975) Intersubjectivity and the transmission of culture, *The Bulletin of the British Psychological Society*, 28: 437–46.

Nunes, T. and Bryant, P. (1996) *Children Doing Mathematics*. Oxford: Blackwell.

Oberhuemer, P. and Ulich, M. (1997) *Working with Young Children in Europe: Provision and Staff Training.* London: Paul Chapman.

Ofsted (2004) *Reading for purpose and pleasure. An evaluation of the teaching of reading in primary schools.* HMI 2393, London: HMSO.

Ogden, L. (1997) *Processes of collaboration in the infant school classroom: their nature and the effects of task structure.* Unpublished PhD thesis, University of Leeds.

Oppenheim, A.N. (1992) *Questionnaire Design, Interviewing and Attitude Measurement.* London: Pinter.

Pahl, K. (1999) *Transformations – Children's Meaning Making in the Nursery.* Stoke on Trent: Trentham Books.

Pahl, K. (2002) Ephemera, mess and miscellaneous piles: texts and practices in families. *Journal of Early Childhood Literacy,* 2 (2): 145–66.

Paley, V.S. (1986) On listening to what the children say, *Harvard Educational Review,* 56: 122–30.

Paley, V.S. (2004) *A Child's Work: The Importance of Fantasy Play.* Chicago, Il.: Chicago University Press.

Pascal, C. (1990) *Under-Fives in Infant Classrooms.* Stoke-on-Trent: Trentham Books.

Pascal, C., Bertram, T. and Ramsden, F. (1997) The effective early learning research project: reflections upon the action during phase 1, *Early Years,* 17 (2): 40–7.

Penn, H. (1999) (ed.) *Theory, Policy and Practice in Early Childhood Services.* Buckingham: Open University Press.

Phillips, T. (1985) Beyond lipservice: discourse development after the age of nine, in G. Wells and J. Nicholls (eds) *Language and Learning: An Instructional Perspective.* Lewes: Falmer.

Pollard, A., Broadfoot, P., Croll, P., Osborn, M. and Abbott, D. (1994) *Changing English Primary Schools: The Impact of the Education Act at Key Stage One.* London: Cassell.

Pugh, G. (1988) *Services for Under Fives: Developing a Co-ordinated Approach.* London: National Children's Bureau.

Pugh, G. (ed.) (2001) *Contemporary Issues in the Early Years: Working Collaboratively for Children.* 3rd edn. London: Paul Chapman Publishing in association with the Coram Family.

Pugh, G. and McQuail, S. (1995) *Effective Organisation of Early Childhood Services: Summary and Strategic Framework.* London: Early Childhood Unit/National Children's Bureau.

QCA (Qualifications and Curriculum Authority) (1998) *A Draft Framework for Qualifications and Training in the Early Years Education, Childcare and Playwork Sector.* London: Qualifications and Curriculum Authority.

QCA (Qualifications and Curriculum Authority) (1999) *The Review of the Desirable Outcomes.* London: Qualifications and Curriculum Authority.

QCA (Qualifications and Curriculum Authority)/ Department of Education and Employment (2000) *Curriculum Guidance for the Foundation
Stage*. London: QCA/DFEE.

QCA (Qualifications and Curriculum Authority)/Department of Education and Employment (2004) *The Foundation Stage Profile Handbook*.
London: QCA.

Rodd, J. (1994) *Leadership in Early Childhood*. Buckingham: Open
University Press.

Rogoff, B. (1990) *Apprenticeships in Thinking: Cognitive Development in
Social Context*. New York: Oxford University Press.

Rogoff, B. (1991) Social interaction as apprenticeship in thinking: guided
participation in spatial planning, in L. Resnick, J. Levine and S.
Teasley (eds) *Perspectives on Socially Shared Cognition*. Washington:
APA.

Rouse, D. (1990) The first three years of life: children trusting,
communicating and learning, in D. Rouse (ed.) *Babies and Toddlers,
Carers and Educators: Quality for Under Threes*. London: National
Children's Bureau.

Saxe, G., Guberman, S. and Gearhart, M. (1987) *Social Processes in Early
Number Development*. Monographs of the Society for Research in
Child Development, serial no. 216, Vol. 52, No. 2.

Schaffer, H.R. (1992) Joint involvement episodes as contexts for
cognitive development, in H. McGurk (ed.) *Childhood and Social
Development: Contemporary Perspectives*. Hove: Lawrence Erlbaum.

Schaffer, H.R. (1996) *Social Development*. Oxford: Blackwell.

Schweinhart, L. and Weikart, D. (1993) *A Summary of Significant Benefits:
The High Scope Perry Pre-School Study Through Age 27*. Ypsilanti, MI:
The High Scope Press.

Scollon, R. and Scollon, B.K. (1981) *Narrative, Literacy and Face in Inter
Ethnic Communication*. New York: Ablex.

Seeger, F., Voigt, J. and Waschescio, U. (eds) (1998) *The Culture of the
Mathematics Classroom*. Cambridge: Cambridge University Press.

Siraj-Blatchford, I. and Sylva, K. (2004) Researching pedagogy in English
pre-schools, *British Educational Research Journal*, 30 (5): 713–30.

Smart, C. and Neale, B. (1999) *Family Fragments*. Cambridge: Polity.

Spodeck, B. (ed.) *Handbook of Research on the Education of Young Children*.
New York: Macmillan.

Stake, R. (1994) Case studies, in N. Denzin and Y. Lincoln (eds) *Handbook
of Qualitative Research*. Thousand Oaks, CA: Sage.

Star, S. L. (1989) The structure of ill-structured solutions: boundary
objects and heterogeneous distributed problem solving, in L. Gasser
and M. N. Huhns (eds) *Readings in Distributed Artificial Intelligence
(Vol 3)*. Menlo Park, CA: Morgan Kaufmann.

Strongin Dodds, L. (1994) Learning together: programmes for parents, *Coordinate*, 39: 12–13.

Sylva, K. (1994) School influences on children's development, *Journal of Child Psychology and Psychiatry*, 35 (1): 135–70.

Sylva, K. (1997) *The Early Years Curriculum: Evidence Based Proposals*. Paper presented at the Schools Curriculum and Assessement Authority conference, Developing the Primary Curriculum: The Next Steps. London: SCAA.

Sylva, K., Melhuish, E., Sammons, P., Siraj-Blatchford, I., Taggart, B. and Elliott, K. (2003) *The Effective Provision of Pre-school Education (EPPE) Project: Findings from the Pre-School Period. Research Brief No. RBX15–03*. London: Department of Education and Skills.

Sylva, K., Siraj-Blatchford, I. and Taggart, B. (2003) *Assessing Quality in the Early Years. Early Childhood Environment Rating Scale: Extension (ECERS-E). Four Curricular Subscales*. Stoke on Trent: Trentham Books.

Sylva, K. and Wiltshire, J. (1993) The impact of early learning on children's later development: a review prepared for the RSA inquiry 'Start Right', *European Early Childhood Research Journal*, 1 (1): 17–40.

Sylva, K., Roy, C. and Painter, M. (1980) *Childwatching at Playgroup and Nursery School*. London: Grant McIntyre.

Taylor, Nelson-Sobres with Aubrey C. (2002) *The Implementation of the Foundation Stage in Reception Classes*. Richmond: Taylor, Nelson-Sobres reported on the DfEE website.

Thompson, I. (ed.) (1997) *Teaching and Learning Early Number*. Buckingham: Open University Press.

Times Educational Supplement (1998) Surestart, 20 November: 5.

Trevarthen, C. (1977) Descriptive analyses of infant communicative behaviour, in H.R. Schaffer (ed.) *Studies in Mother Infant Interaction*. London: Academic Press.

Trevarthen, C. (1993) The functions of emotions in early infant communication and development, in J. Nadel and L. Camaiori (eds) *New Perspectives on Early Communicative Development*. London: Routledge.

Trevarthen, C. (2000) Early Childhood Brain Research: Keynote address for BAECE/OMEP National Brainwaves Conference, Warwick University, November 2000.

Tunstill, J., Meadows, P., Allnock, D., Akhurst, S., Chrysanthou, S., Garbers, C., Morley, A., van de Velde, T. (January 2005) *Implementing Sure Start Local Programmes: An In Depth Study*. NESS at Birkbeck College London for the Sure Start Unit. Nottingham: DfES Publications.

Tymms, P. (1999) *Baseline Assessment and Monitoring in Primary Schools: Achievements, Attitudes and Value-added Indicators*. London: David Fulton.

van Oers, B. (1996) Are you sure?: stimulating mathematical thinking during young children's play, *European Early Childhood Education Research Journal*, 4 (1): 71–87.

van Oers, B. (1999) Teaching opportunities in play, in M. Hedegaard and J. Lompscher (eds) *Learning, Activity and Development*. Aarhus: Aarhus University Press.

van Oers, B. and Hännikäinen, M. (2001) Some thoughts about togetherness: an introduction, *International Journal of Early Years Education*, 9 (2): 101–8.

Wade, B. (1993) Story at home and school, *Educational Review: Occasional Publications, No. 10*. Birmingham: University of Birmingham.

Warin, J. (2001) Joined-up services for young children and their families: papering over the cracks or re-constructing the foundations. Paper delivered at BERA 2001, University of Leeds. Available on Education-line website, University of Leeds.

Weinberger, J. (1996) *Literacy Goes to School*. London: Paul Chapman Publishing.

Weinberger, J., Hannon, P. and Nutbrown, C. (1990) *Ways of Working with Parents to Promote Literacy Development*. Sheffield: University of Sheffield Division of Education.

Wells, G. (1987) *The Meaning Makers: Children Learning Language and Using Language to Learn*. London: Heinemann Educational.

Wertsch, J. (1991) A sociocultural approach to socially shared cognition, in L. Resnick, J. Levine and S. Teasley (eds) *Perspectives on Socially Shared Cognition*. Washington: APA.

Wertsch, J. (1997) Collective memory: issues from a sociocultural perspective, in M. Cole, Y. Engestrom and O. Vasquez (eds) *Mind, Culture and Activity*. Cambridge: Cambridge University Press.

Wertsch, J., Del Rio, P. and Alvarez, A. (eds) (1995) *Sociocultural Studies of Mind*. Cambridge: Cambridge University Press.

Whitehead, M.R. (1990) *Language and Literacy in the Early Years: An Approach for Education Students*. London: Paul Chapman.

Wilkinson, J.E. (1994) *Flagships: An Evaluation/Research Study of Community Nurseries in Strathclyde Region 1989–92*. Glasgow: Department of Education, University of Glasgow.

Wilkinson, K. (2003) Children's favourite books, *Journal of Early Childhood Literacy*, 3 (3): 275–301.

Wollman-Bonilla, J.E. (2001) Family involvement in early writing instruction, *Journal of Early Childhood Literacy*, 1 (2): 167–92.

Wood, D. (1986) Aspects of teaching and learning, in M. Richards and P. Light (eds) *Children of Social Worlds*. Cambridge: Polity Press.

Wood, D. (1988) *How Children Think and Learn*. Oxford: Blackwell.

Woodhead, M., Faulkner, D. and Littleton, K. (eds) (1998) *Cultural Worlds of Early Childhood*. London: Routledge.

Author Index

Subject Index